IPSWICH TO FELIXSTOWE BRANCH

THROUGH TIME

Andy T. Wallis

AMBERLEY PUBLISHING

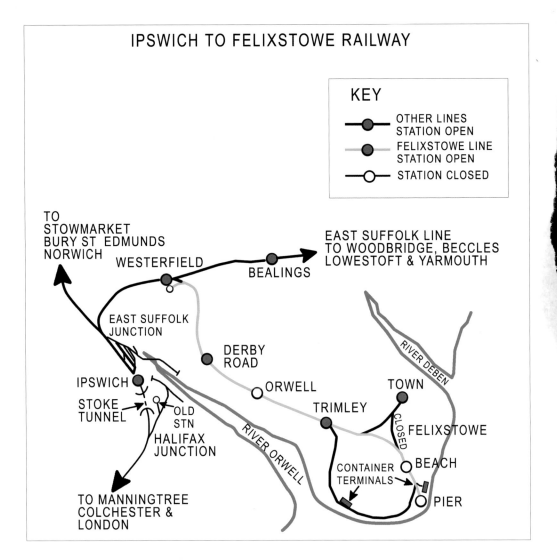

IPSWICH TO FELIXSTOWE RAILWAY

KEY

OTHER LINES
STATION OPEN

FELIXSTOWE LINE
STATION OPEN

STATION CLOSED

TO
STOWMARKET
BURY ST EDMUNDS
NORWICH

WESTERFIELD

BEALINGS

EAST SUFFOLK LINE
TO WOODBRIDGE, BECCLES
LOWESTOFT & YARMOUTH

EAST SUFFOLK
JUNCTION

DERBY
ROAD

RIVER DEBEN

IPSWICH

ORWELL

TOWN

STOKE
TUNNEL

OLD
STN

TRIMLEY

CLOSED

FELIXSTOWE

HALIFAX
JUNCTION

RIVER ORWELL

CONTAINER
TERMINALS

BEACH

TO MANNINGTREE
COLCHESTER &
LONDON

PIER

First published 2012

Amberley Publishing
The Hill, Stroud
Gloucestershire, GL5 4EP

www.amberley-books.com

Copyright © Andy T. Wallis, 2012

The right of Andy T. Wallis to be identified as the
Author of this work has been asserted in accordance
with the Copyrights, Designs and Patents Act 1988.

ISBN 978 1 4456 0766 5

British Library Cataloguing in Publication Data.
A catalogue record for this book is available from
the British Library.

Typeset in 9.5pt on 12pt Celeste.
Typesetting by Amberley Publishing.
Printed in the UK.

Introduction

The Eastern Union Railway reached Ipswich from Colchester in June 1846, to a temporary terminus south of Stoke Hill, after the Eastern Counties Railway had failed to complete their London to Norwich line. The EUR line from Ipswich to Bury St Edmunds followed in November 1846, and, with the completion of the tunnel under Stoke Hill, enabled Bury trains to use the temporary Ipswich terminus until the new station north of the tunnel opened in 1860.

The East Suffolk line began life as the Halesworth, Beccles & Haddiscoe Railway in 1851 and was opened to passenger traffic from 4 December 1854. A name change followed in 1854, along with an authorized extension to Woodbridge, where it was to meet the EUR line from East Suffolk Junction through Westerfield to Woodbridge. This scheme had been authorized in 1847, but had to wait until 1854, when the powers were renewed for construction. The line opened throughout on 1 June 1859.

The actual Felixstowe branch was the idea of Colonel George Tomline, a prominent local landowner, and was authorized by Act of Parliament on 19 July 1875. Named originally as the Felixstowe Railway and Pier Company, a further act authorized a name change to the Felixstowe Railway and Dock Company. The line opened to passenger traffic on 1 May 1877, running between Westerfield and Felixstowe Pier, being single throughout, with intermediate stations at Derby Road (Ipswich) and Orwell and Felixstowe (later Beach). A passing loop was provided at Orwell – the station at Orwell was provided to serve Colonel Tomline's Orwell Park estate.

The Great Eastern Railway ran the line from 1 September 1879; purchase followed in 1887, when the original company changed its name to the Felixstowe Dock and Railway Company, retaining control of the docks. At the same time, powers were obtained to provide a station at Trimley, which was built on Colonel Tomline's land and duly opened after some delay on 1 May 1891. A further act in 1893 allowed the GER to build a spur east of Trimley to a new station, to be named Felixstowe Town, and a further spur from the town station back towards the original line at the newly named Felixstowe Beach station. The direct line, which formed the third side of the triangle of routes, was closed and lifted.

Felixstowe Town was provided with a large, new station, a goods yard, and a new signal box with plenty of spare levers, allowing for future expansion. Extra land was retained between the original platform and goods yard for an additional island platform, which was provided by the London and North Eastern Railway in 1938.

There was talk of doubling the line back in the LNER days, but this came to nothing, principally due to the Second World War. After heavy use during the war, which included the use of the docks and harbour by the Royal Navy, the facilities were run down and silted up. The Pier passenger station was temporarily closed as a wartime measure in September 1939; it reopened in the summer of 1946, only to close completely in July 1951.

The Docks had been allowed to silt up during the war period, and never recovered much traffic until purchased outright by Mr Gordon Parker in 1951. By 1957, some 87,000 tons of cargo was being handled; this increased further to over 600,000 in 1965. On the branch stations, the passenger service reached its zenith during the 1950s. Orwell, never a busy station but useful for crossing purposes, was closed from June 1959 and the crossing loop was taken out of use. This was to play havoc with the long single-line section between Derby Road and Trimley many years later. The Beach station was, by the 1960s, being used during the summer timetable. The station closed completely at the beginning of the 1967 winter timetable.

Reinstatement of the direct line to the docks came in May 1970. Felixstowe Town station was reduced to a single platform face from that time, although some reduction in facilities had taken place in the 1960s. Staff were withdrawn in September 1966, when conductor guards were introduced on the DMU services. The Dock Company built a new container depot, which opened in November 1972, services being handled by Freightliner.

With freight traffic booming in the 1980s, a new terminal was opened at Felixstowe North, and, to save a journey through the docks, a direct line was built from Trimley to the new facility. This opened in March 1987. Further freight and passenger growth meant that, in 1999, Railtrack resignalled the line throughout and lengthened the passing loop at Derby Road, this allowing two full-length Freightliner trains to pass at this location.

With a rosy future assured, surely electrification and the promised part-doubling of the line will take place?

ATW
May 2012

Ipswich

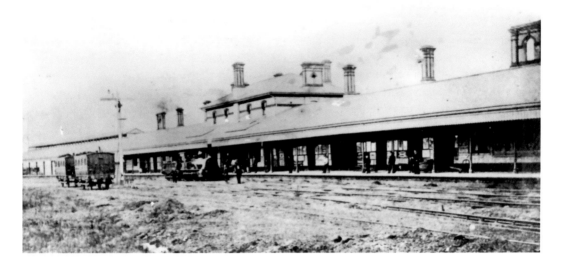

A very old early view of the original station at Ipswich, taken before the island platform was built in 1869; the ornate chimneys survived when seen on the lower view. (HMRS)

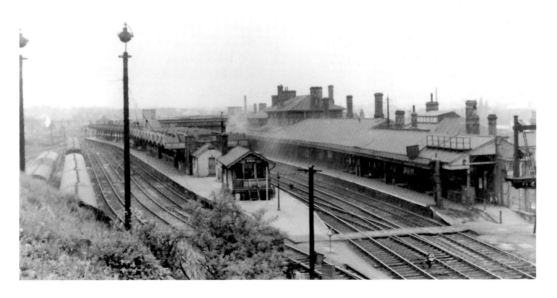

A view from Stoke Hill looking down on Ipswich station, taken in steam days, with the carriage sidings on the left and the station signal box in the centre of the view. The main buildings are located on the Up platform. Note the through line between the platforms. This view was taken on 14 May 1956. (H. C. Casserley)

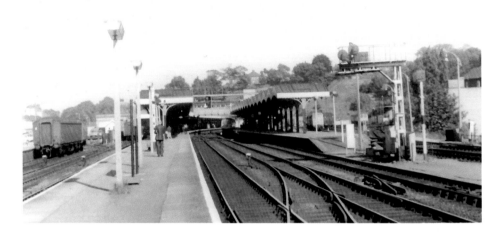

General view of Ipswich station, looking towards Colchester and London from the main Up platform, as seen 7 June 1969. The Felixstowe branch trains tended to start from the bay platform on the left of this view. (H. C. Casserley)

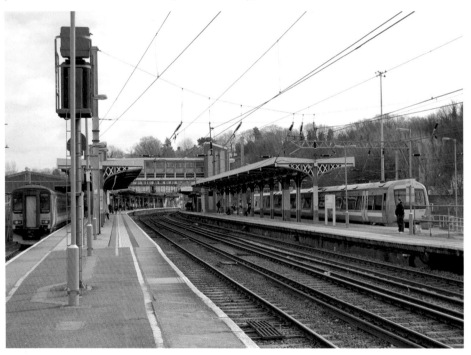

Today's view taken from a similar position shows many changes, including a modernised footbridge and track layout. The semaphore signalling has been swept away and the station is equipped with full bidirectional signalling, now all controlled from Colchester Area Signalling Centre. (Ray Bishop)

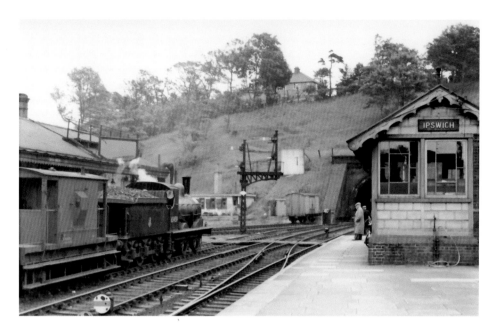

LNER Class J15 stands at the Up main platform at Ipswich, with a short freight train awaiting the signal to proceed. At this time the signalling was all controlled from several local signal boxes. Ipswich station signal box can be seen on the right of this view, which was taken on 9 June 1956. (R. C. Riley/Transport Treasury)

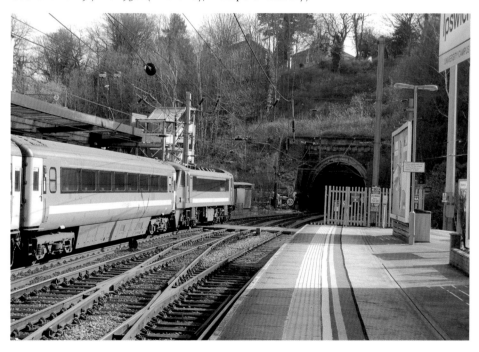

A Class 90, hauling mark 3 coaches, departs towards Colchester and London. Stoke Hill tunnel can be seen behind the modern security fence. The structure above the locomotive is the stairway to and from the multi-storey car park. (Ray Bishop)

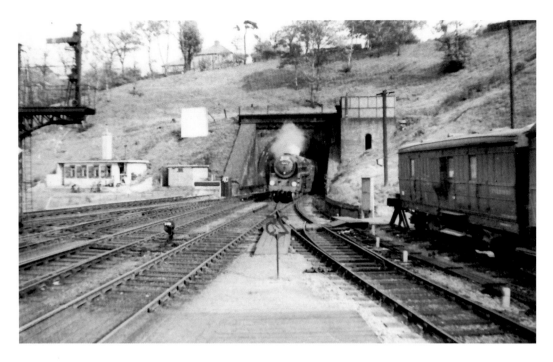

Britannia Class locomotive No. 70xxx bursts out of Stoke Hill tunnel to arrive at the London end of the Down platform at Ipswich in the 1950s. (Stations UK)

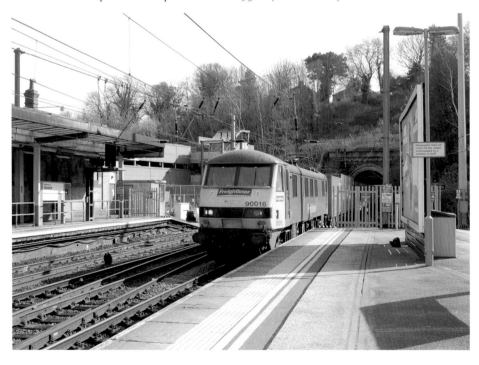

Today, a Class 90 electric locomotive, No. 90016, enters the station on a Down Freightliner working to Felixstowe. This train will go into Ipswich yard for the locomotive to be exchanged for the trip down the branch, which is not electrified – yet. (Ray Bishop)

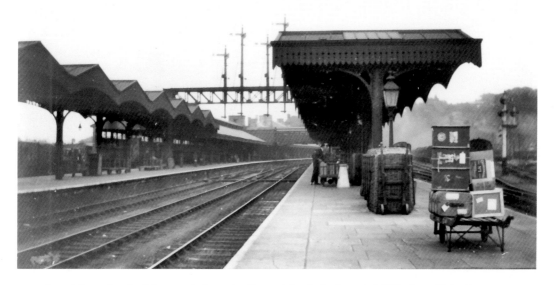

Ipswich station, looking south from the Down island platform in LNER days. This view was taken in 1928. Note the trolley full of luggage waiting to be loaded onto the next train. The lower quadrant semaphores in the middle of the station had yet to be replaced by colour light signalling. (Stations UK)

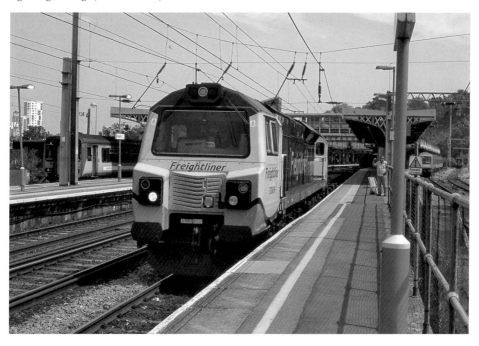

A similar view today shows the latest diesel freight locomotive, Class 70009, waiting at the Down main platform at Ipswich. The canopy has received a new flat roof since the earlier picture. The columns and supports are the originals. (Ray Bishop)

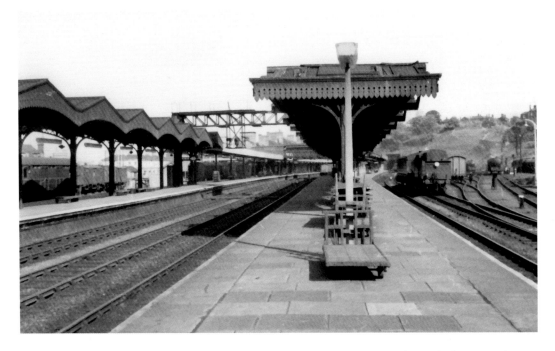

Another view taken from the Down platform, showing the yard on the right, with the original canopy on both platforms. However, the fine lower quadrant semaphores seen in the 1928 view have been replaced by a searchlight signal. (Stations UK)

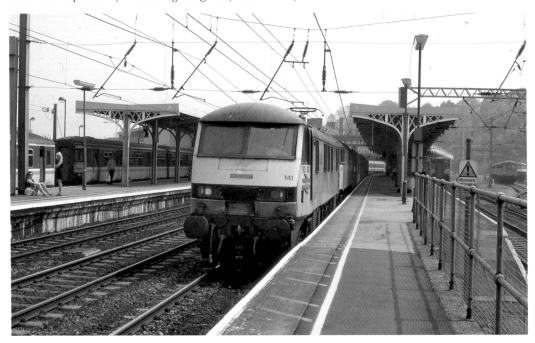

Moving forward some forty years, all has changed again, with a platform extension, new canopy roofs, overhead power cables, and a double-headed train featuring Class 90141 and Class 47337. This view was taken on 17 May 1997. (Ray Bishop)

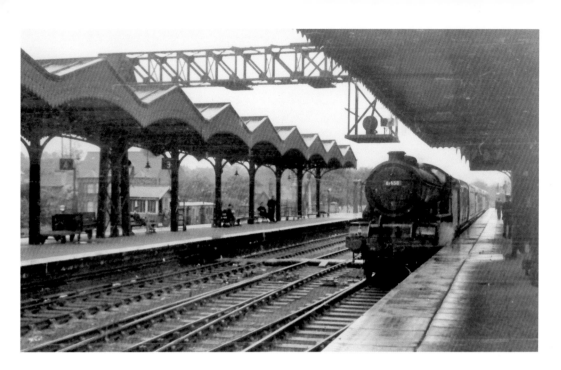

Locomotive Class B17 named *The Essex Regiment* No. 61658 stands at the country end of the Up platform at Ipswich in 1953, with a local passenger train. The replacement searchlight signal mentioned previously can be seen above the locomotive. (Stations UK)

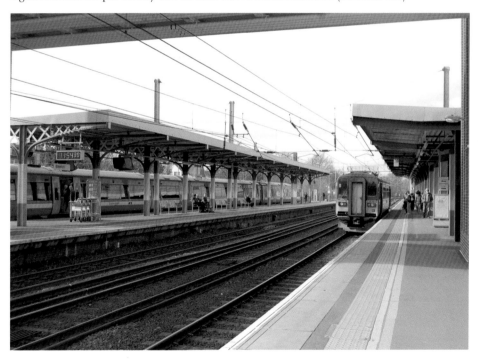

Today, the same view features a single-coach Class 153 diesel unit, awaiting its next working to Felixstowe. These units normally work the local passenger service. (Ray Bishop)

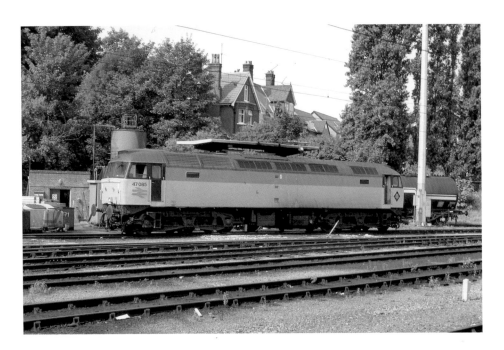

A Class 47 diesel seen at Ipswich fuelling point awaits its next turn of duty. Originally, the Class 47s were introduced in the 1960s as a passenger-hauling locomotive, but in later years could be seen hauling freight trains as well. 47085 is seen in two-tone grey livery on 1 August 1992. (Ray Bishop)

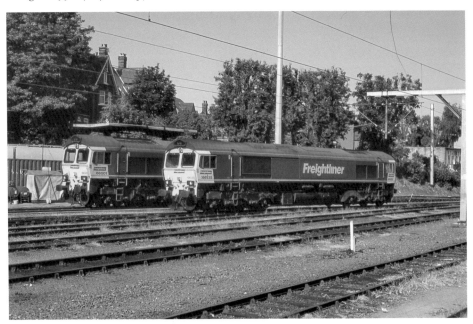

Moving forward nearly twenty years, we see a pair of Freightliner liveried Class 66 at the Ipswich stabling/fuelling point. The locomotives featured are 66501 and 66535. The common feature in both photographs is the house in the trees, overlooking the yard. (Ray Bishop)

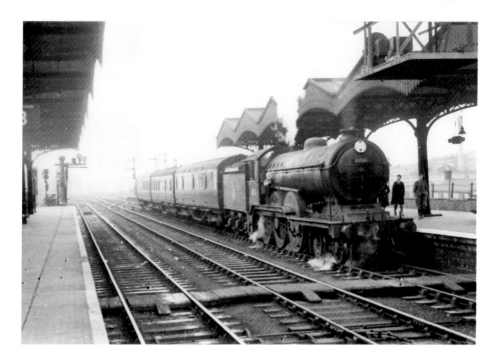

Locomotive Class B12 No. 61561 stands at the country end of the Up platform at Ipswich with a three-coach local service. The engine is blowing off excess steam, waiting to depart. (Stations UK)

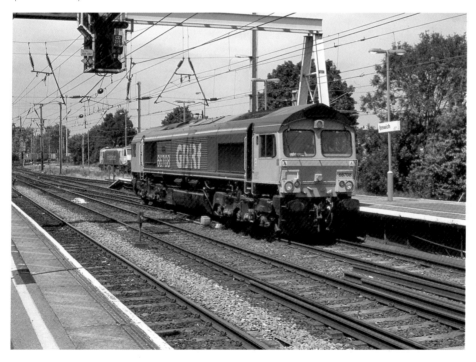

Over a half-century later, we see a Class 66 freight locomotive in GB Rail Freight livery running round its train at Ipswich during 2011. (Ray Bishop)

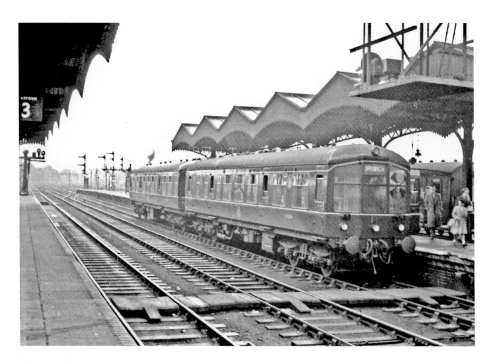

Derby Lightweight-type DMU Nos E79044 and E79260 stand at Ipswich on a local passenger service, as seen on 28 July 1956. The semaphores seen in the background were to last many more years, until the station was remodelled and resignalled prior to electrification in the 1980s. (Brian Pask)

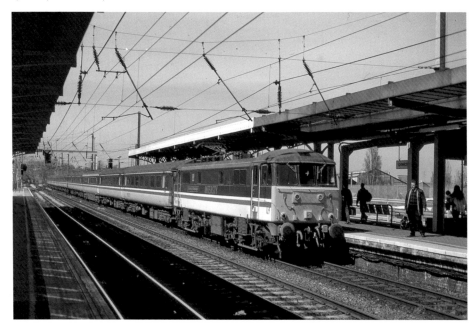

Class 86237 arrives with the 12.05 Norwich to Liverpool Street express passenger service on 23 April 1995. The semaphore signalling has been replaced and the overhead power lines dominate the scene. (Ray Bishop)

Ipswich Goods Yards
and Dock Lines

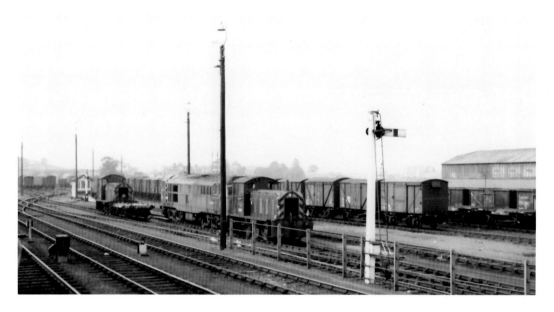

Two small Class 04 shunters and a Class 31 diesel are seen in Ipswich upper goods yard. Plenty of wagons can be seen in the background, indicating healthy levels of traffic. The signal in the foreground protects the line leading down to the lower goods yard. (Dr I. C. Allen/Transport Treasury)

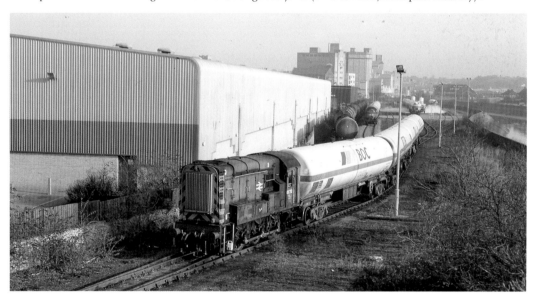

Happier days at Ipswich lower yard, with BOC tanker traffic being shunted by 08752. This view was taken on 17 January 1992. Now the yard has been closed and the track has been lifted – no doubt the area will be redeveloped. (Ray Bishop)

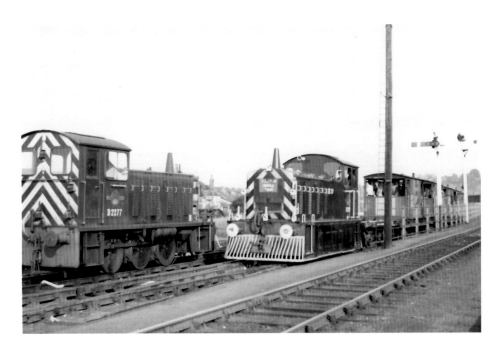

A D2281 Class 04 shunter and match wagon hauls a train of brake vans, being run for an Ipswich Transport Society special train. Seen here topping the grade up from the lower yard and quayside into the upper yard, passing fellow Class 04 shunter D2277. (Dr I. C. Allen/Transport Treasury)

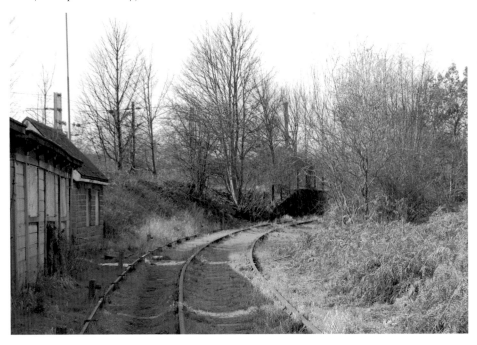

The line to the lower yard is now out of use pending lifting. This view is taken further down the branch. The retaining wall and railings in this view are the same ones seen in the top picture adjacent to the brake vans. (Ray Bishop)

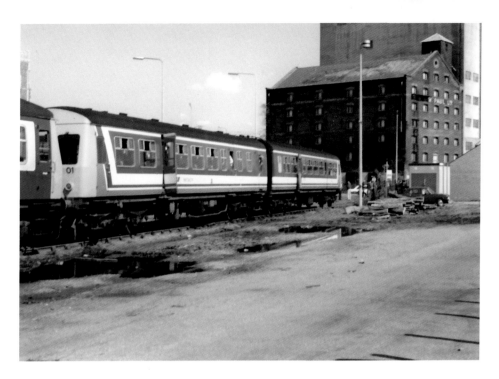

Branch Line Society's rail tour of 1989 visited the railways around Ipswich as well as Felixstowe. The 2x2 car Metro-Camel DMU forming the special train is seen standing in Ipswich lower goods yard, adjacent to the level crossing. (Andy T. Wallis)

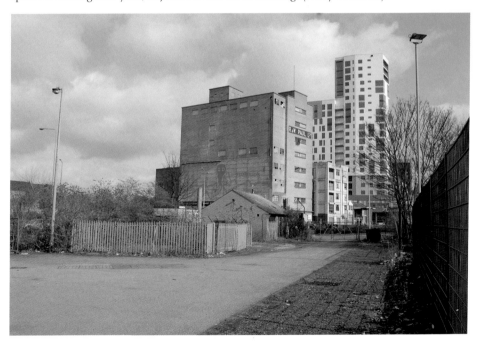

Today the rails have gone and the land is awaiting development. The level crossing is now closed and the R&W Paul Ltd building has a flat roof now. (Ray Bishop)

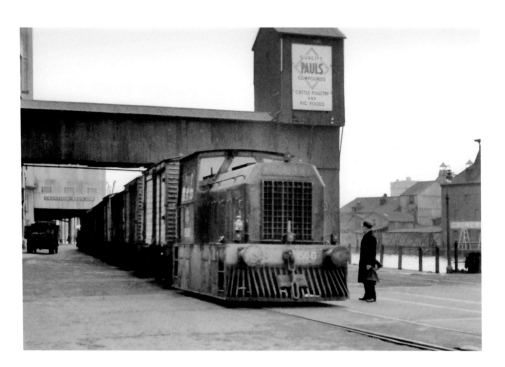

A local docks shunter is seen hauling a train of closed vans, adjacent to the level crossing leading to the lower yard. Paul's processing mills was the building to the left of the train, and used to send out and receive much traffic by rail. (D. Lawrence/*Photos from the Fifties*)

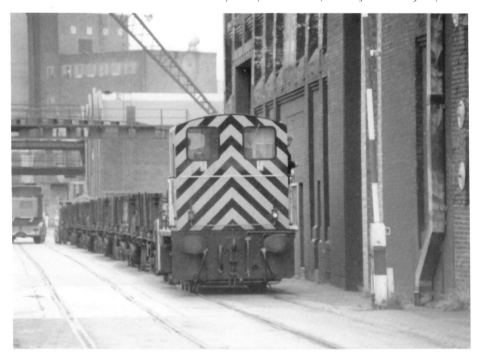

Class 03 shunter No. 03089, working on the quayside lines with a rake of wagons. Today there is no rail traffic to the quayside or lower yard. (Paul Lemon)

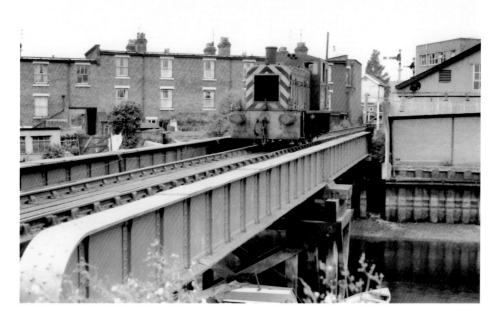

Class 03 shunter D2051 crosses the river Orwell on the line connecting the upper goods yard to the lower goods yard and the quayside. The signals in the distance protect the adjacent level crossing. The signal box can be seen to the right of the buildings. (Dr I. C. Allen/Transport Treasury)

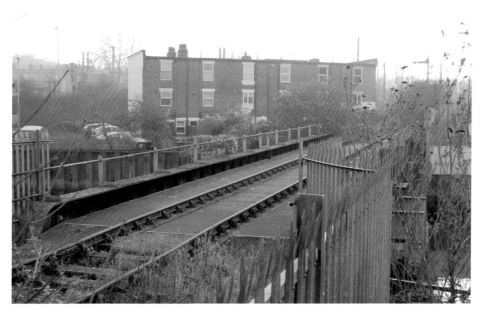

Today the line to the lower yard is closed and most of the rails have already been lifted, except for the section over the river bridge. The flats in the background have been reduced in size during the preceding years. The signal box has gone, but the semaphore signal still stands guard at the level crossing. (Ray Bishop)

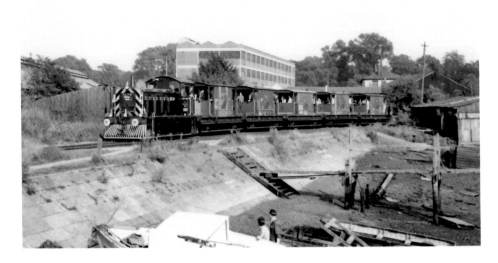

An Ipswich Transport Society brake van tour, hauled by Class 04 shunter D2281, down the goods only branch to the lower yard and onto the quayside. At this time the rails went to the local power station. The returning trip can be seen arriving in the upper yard on page 16. (Dr I. C. Allen/Transport Treasury)

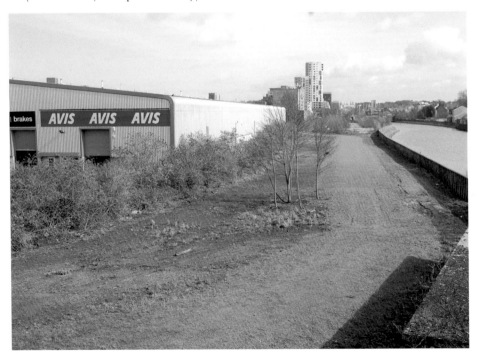

Today all the rails have gone, the whole area having been redeveloped. This view is looking back towards the lower yard. (Ray Bishop)

Ipswich East Suffolk Junction

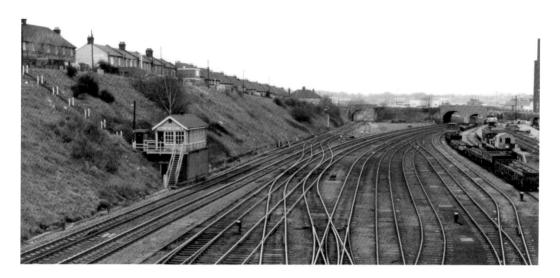

East Suffolk Junction, seen from the adjacent road bridge before the area was modernised. At this time there were four main tracks from the junction into Ipswich station, plus the double junction into the goods yard. The East Suffolk line is seen curving away under the arched bridge on the right. (David Underwood)

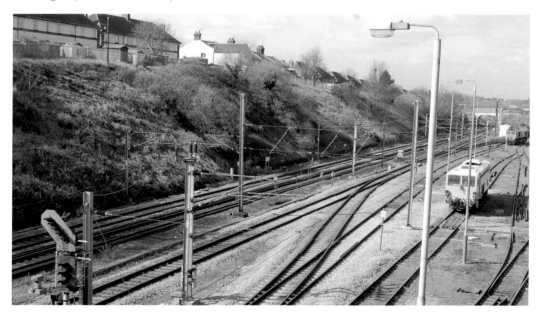

Today the whole area has been simplified, with the East Suffolk line being singled from the junction, and the connections into the goods yard reduced to single leads. The signalling has been renewed, and the old signal box closed and demolished. (Ray Bishop)

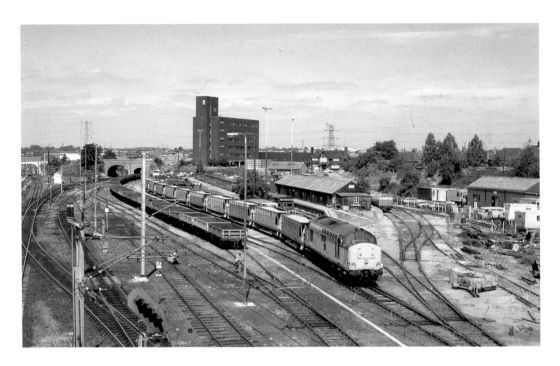

Even in its reduced form, the goods yard is still busy. This view, taken on 6 August 1995, sees a Class 37 hauling a train of granite ballast for the civil engineers' use. The East Suffolk line can be seen turning away under the bridge at the top left of the picture. (Ray Bishop)

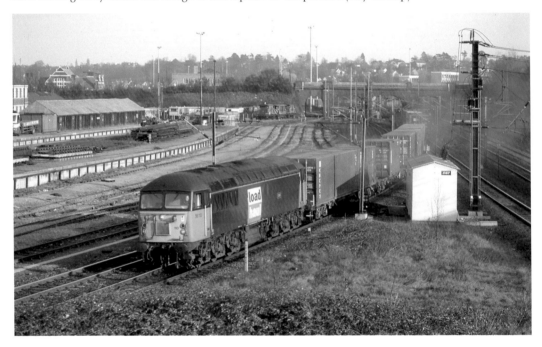

A wide selection of motive power has been seen on Felixstowe traffic over the last forty years or so, ranging from pairs of Class 37s to Class 47s. In the 1990s, it was the turn of the Class 56. This view is of 56110 departing from Ipswich en route to Felixstowe, as seen on 4 April 1996. (Ray Bishop)

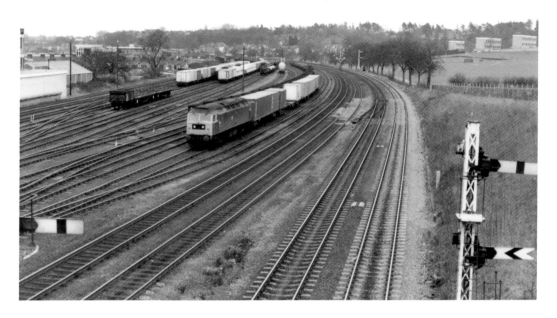

This view looks south from the road overbridge towards Ipswich station. The area is controlled by semaphore signals worked from East Suffolk Junction signal box. (David Underwood)

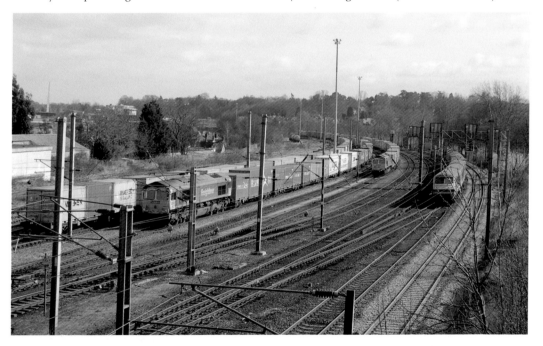

Today a similar view sees a local service heading towards Ipswich on the main line, with two Freightliner trains waiting to depart in the goods yard. The whole area has been resignalled, and overhead power lines dominate the view. Several sidings in the goods yard have been lifted in this view. (Ray Bishop)

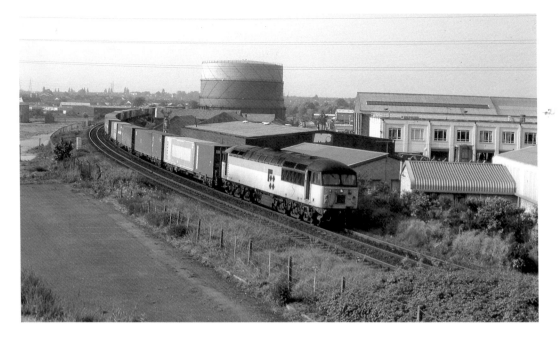

A Class 56 hauling a Freightliner service approaches East Suffolk Junction with the 16.46 Felixstowe South to Coatbridge service, as seen on 12 May 1998. There are plans to put an east to north curve in at this location to avoid the need to change ends with the locomotive in Ipswich yard. (Ray Bishop)

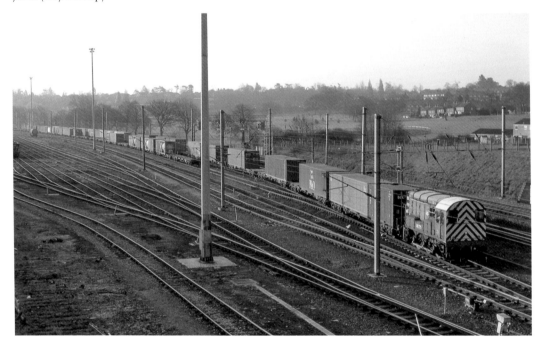

Certain trains travel from Felixstowe to Ipswich yard, only waiting to be joined with other traffic before proceeding on their journey. Here we see Class diesel 08755 shunting the yard at the East Suffolk end, making up a train. This view was taken on 18 April 1996. (Ray Bishop)

Westerfield

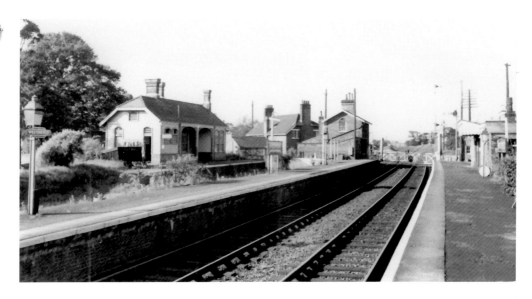

A neat and tidy view taken in 1967, looking towards Ipswich and showing the original Felixstowe Railway and Dock Company building minus canopy on the left. The crossing keeper's house is next to the level crossing, shown here with the gates across the railway. (Stations UK)

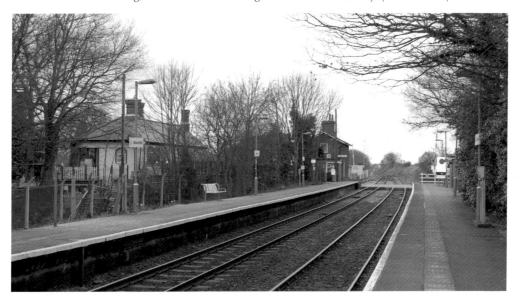

Today the view has not changed a lot. The former Felixstowe Railway building has been sold off and is now a private house. For many years it was kept boarded up, except for the toilet, which was used by the signalman. This practice ceased when modern facilities were built adjacent to the signal box. (Ray Bishop)

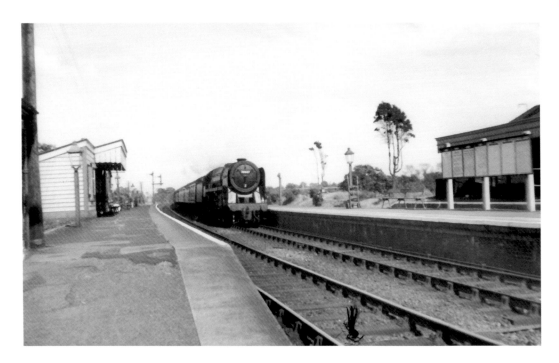

Class 7P Britannia pacific locomotive No. 70007 at the head of an Up express. This view was taken from the Down platform ramp adjacent to the level crossing. (Stations UK)

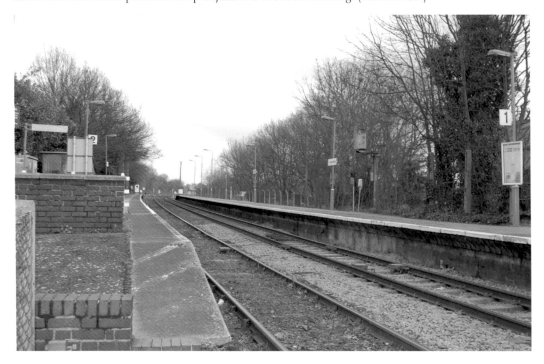

Today the same view shows the platforms with modern lighting and name boards. Trees have been planted behind the platform edge as screening. The Down platform shelter has been replaced with a bus type shelter. (Ray Bishop)

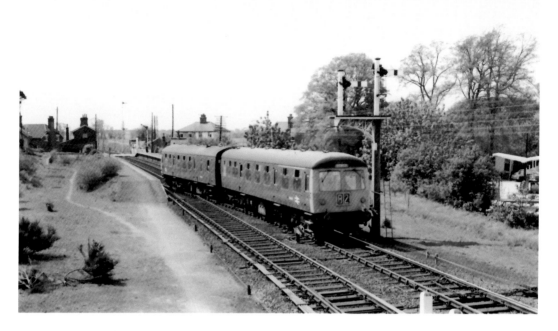

A Cravens Class 105 DMU shunts from the Down to the Up line at Westerfield, this view was taken from the adjacent signal box, date not known. (Dr I. C. Allen/Transport Treasury)

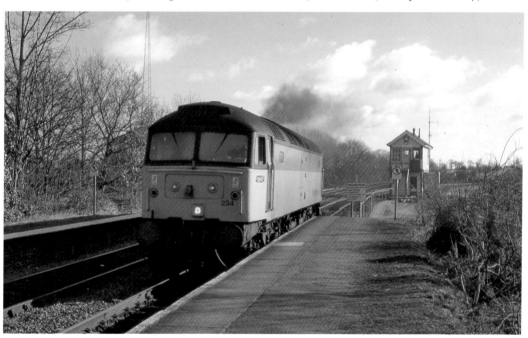

Unable to replicate the previous view due to the signal box having been closed and demolished, we have instead locomotive 47234 returning from Felixstowe, light engine passing through the Up platform. All Felixstowe trains to and from now use this line, as the junction was singled some years previously. (Ray Bishop)

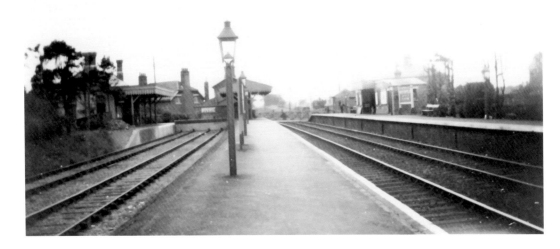

An early LNER view of the station, as seen from the Ipswich end of the Up platform. The original Felixstowe station building still had its canopy intact at this time, along with its short platform. Covered accommodation was also supplied on the main platforms. (Stations UK)

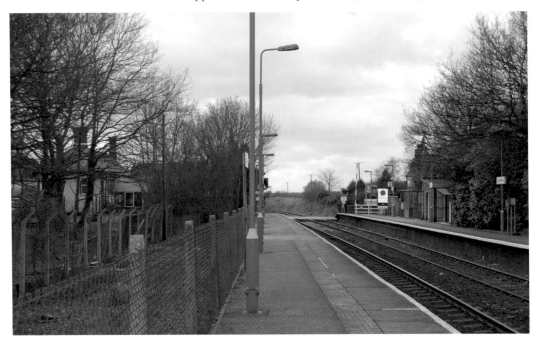

The view today shows a basic functional unstaffed station with modern lighting. The former Felixstowe bay lines have long been lifted and the land sold off, together with the original station building. (Ray Bishop)

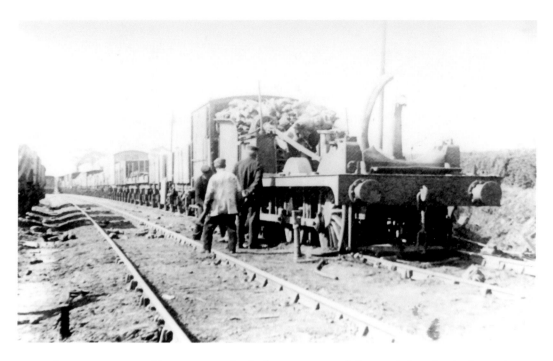

The consequences of low water in the boiler, or just metal fatigue, led to this boiler explosion at the top of a bank near Westerfield station. The destruction was total. This view was dated 25 September 1900. (HMRS ABA533)

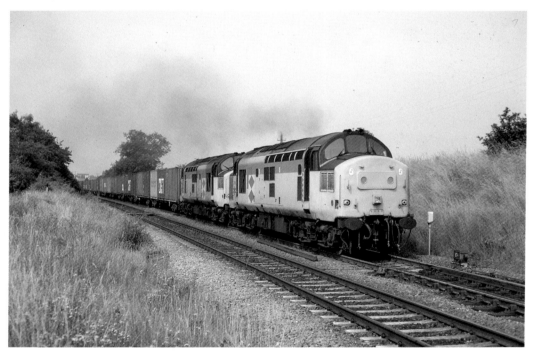

Over nine decades later, 37178 and 37218 arrive safely at Westerfield, ready to cross over onto the Felixstowe branch. This train is the 03.35 Stratford to Felixstowe North service. (Ray Bishop)

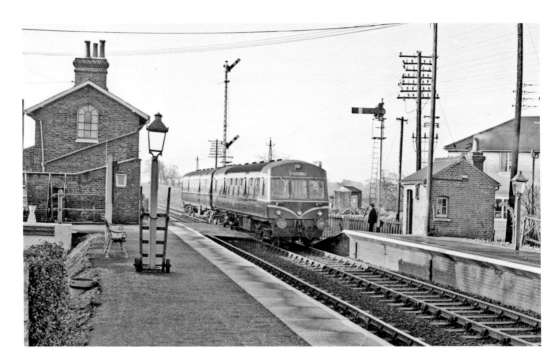

A Met/Camel DMU arrives at the station with a Felixstowe working on 2 December 1961. Note the co-acting Down home signal above the train. The signal on the right is actually the Up starting signal, placed on the right for sighting purposes. (Brian Pask)

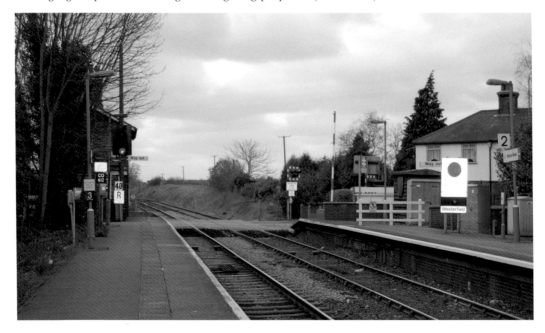

The semaphore signals and manual level crossing gates have long gone, as has the crossing keeper's hut. A modern signal protects the crossing, while on the other platform a Stop Board marks the end of RETB working on the East Suffolk line. Tree growth partially obscures the station building. (Ray Bishop)

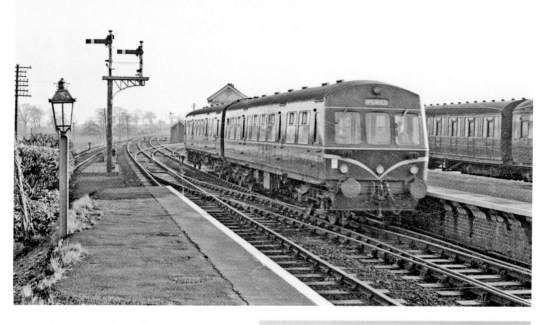

Above: A Met/Camel DMU arrives on the Up platform with a Felixstowe to Ipswich service, seen on 2 December 1961. The former Felixstowe bay platforms have spare rolling stock berthed in them. At this time the station was illuminated with old-style gas lights, and the concrete and wooden bracket signal stood guard over the junction. (Brian Pask)

Right: A Class 47 hauled Freightliner train passes Westerfield signal box during 1987. The layout by this time had been simplified, and the bracket signal was out of use, shorn of its arms. (Andy T. Wallis)

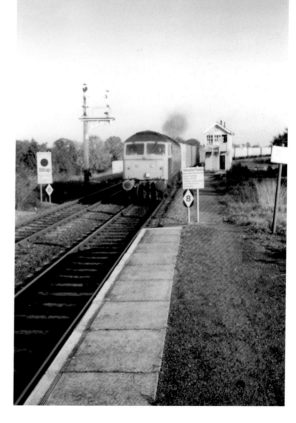

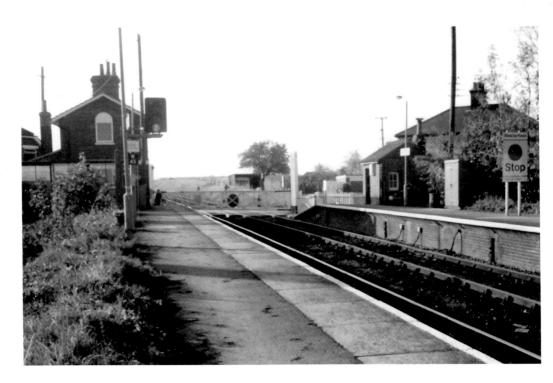

Westerfield in 1987, looking towards Ipswich. The Down co-acting signal had been replaced with a colour light signal, as had the semaphore Up starter, with W43 now a three-aspect colour light signal. At this time the level crossing was still manual, gates operated by a crossing keeper. (Andy T. Wallis)

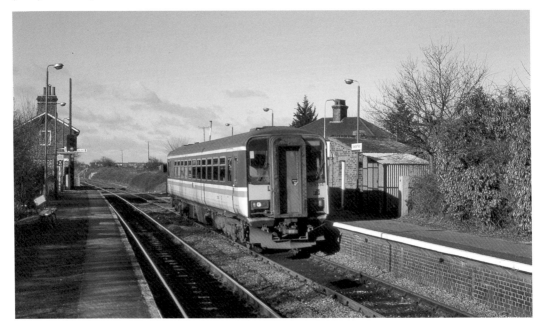

Today, a single-car Class 153 diesel unit arrives on the Down platform on a Lowestoft working. All Felixstowe services now use the opposite platform. (Ray Bishop)

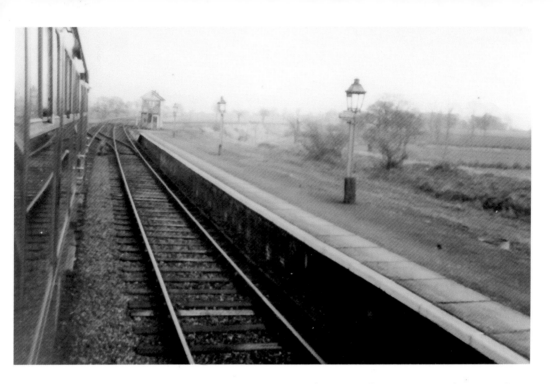

Leaning out of the window of a local DMU service, this view taken on 4 December 1966 shows the lamps on the Up platform and the signal box, with the Felixstowe branch curving away to the right in the distance. (Dickie Pearce)

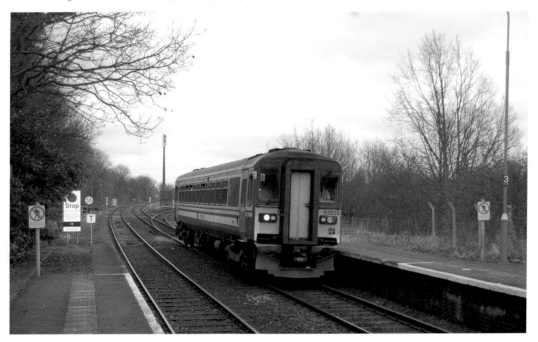

A Class 153 single-coach diesel unit arrives on the Up platform with a service from Felixstowe. Most Felixstowe services are formed of these units. (Ray Bishop)

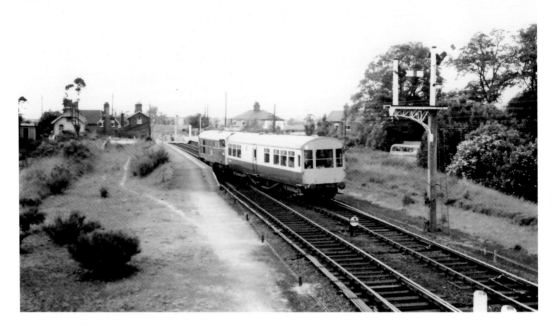

Two views of an Officers Inspection train being propelled. The first is of the train being propelled over the trailing crossover at Westerfield, with the train being signalled down the East Suffolk line. By this time the Felixstowe bay platform lines had all been lifted. The lower view is of the train being propelled down the Felixstowe line with the Inspection saloon, leading motive power being provided by Brush type 2, later Class 31 diesel. (Dr I. C. Allen/ Transport Treasury)

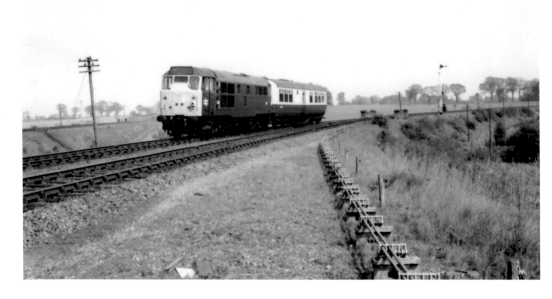

Derby Road

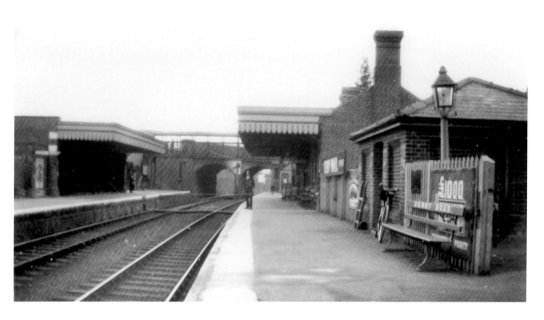

A very early LNER view of Derby Road station, taken from the Down platform, looking towards Westerfield. At this time the station had full facilities, with station buildings and canopies on both platforms. Note the station name on the platform seat. (Stations UK)

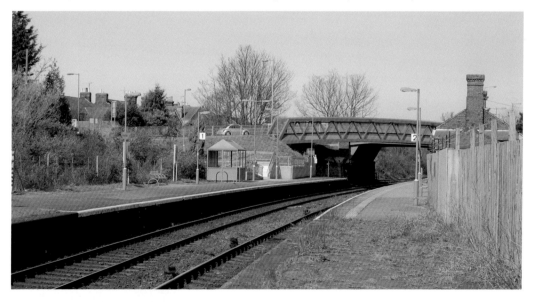

Today, all the buildings have been demolished or sold off for other uses. A new footbridge has been installed. Note that only the used parts of the platforms are maintained. (Ray Bishop)

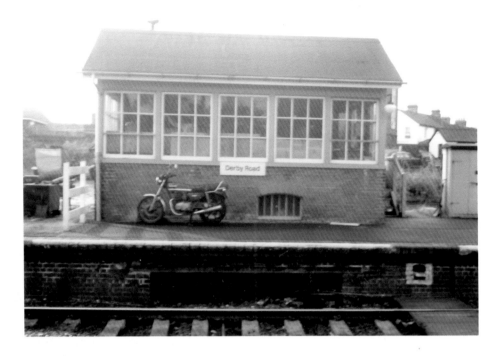

Derby Road signal box, as seen in 1987. This station was the principal crossing place on the branch after the crossing loop shut at Trimley. A siding, serving a coal yard and scrap merchants, trailed into the Up loop to the left of the signal box. Note the signalman's motorbike parked outside the box. (Andy T. Wallis)

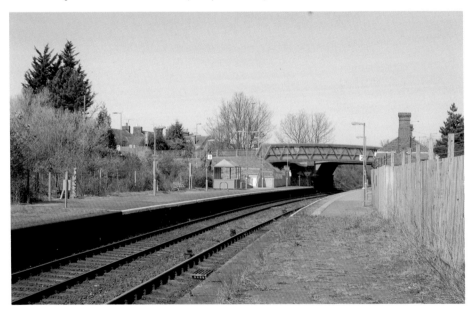

Today all has changed, with the signal box closed and demolished, and all the station buildings removed or sold off for other uses. The road overbridge has been rebuilt to allow larger containers to use the route. The signal box was located left of the lamp post at the edge of the weed-free platform. (Ray Bishop)

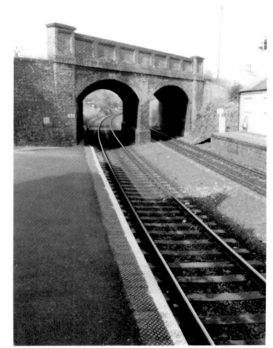

The road overbridge, with its two archways at the Westerfield end of the station, seen here in 1987. The Up starting signal, seen through the left-hand arch, was previously located adjacent to the bridge, between the two tracks. (Andy T. Wallis)

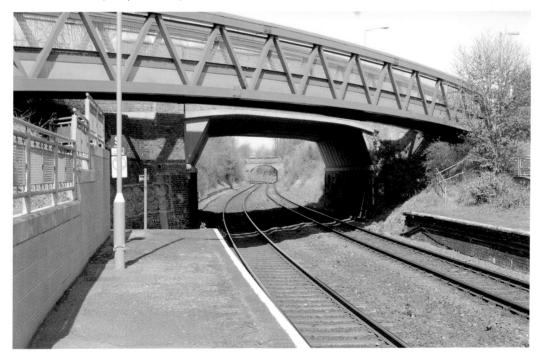

Today the rebuilt overbridge can be clearly seen with the adjacent footbridge, as can the extended passing loop, which continues just beyond the next bridge. (Ray Bishop)

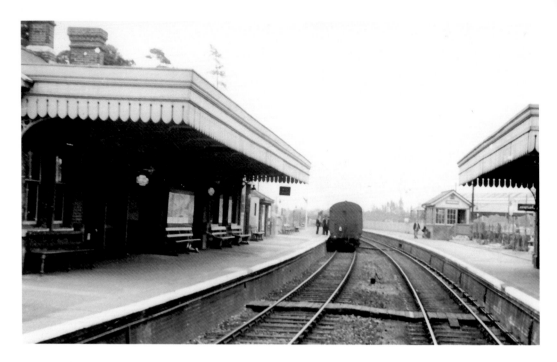

A Down local branch train is seen leaving the station. This view was taken from track level on 14 May 1956, a time when the station had full facilities and staff to keep it neat and tidy. (H. C. Casserley)

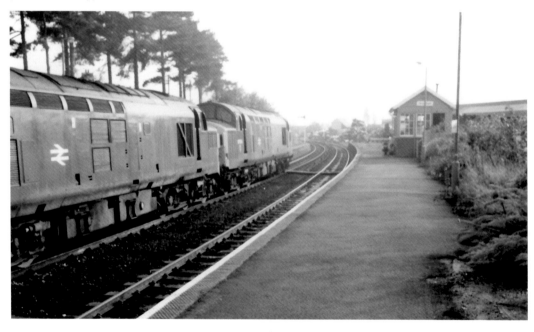

Some thirty years later, a pair of Class 37s on a Freightliner working wait adjacent to the signal box for the Up local service to arrive and clear the single line to Trimley. At this time, the loop was not long enough to pass two full-length freight trains. Note the absence of the canopy, though the signal box acts as a marker for comparison purposes. (Andy T. Wallis)

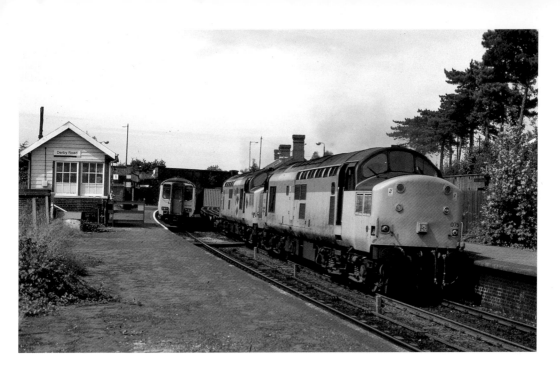

The modern view first shows Classes 37075 and 37131, waiting to proceed to Felixstowe North terminal with a Freightliner service train that had originated at Crew. This view was taken on 1 August 1992. (Ray Bishop)

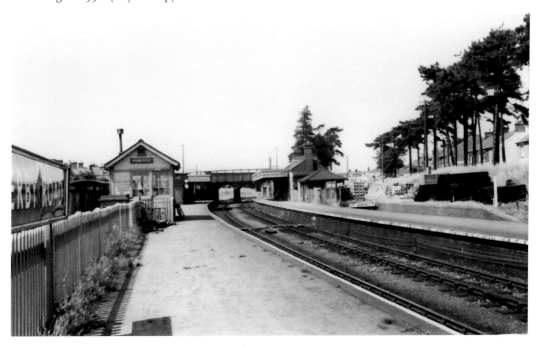

Some twenty-five years earlier, the same view shows the trees and the signal box with a different chimney and name board. The weeds in this view are nothing compared to the top view. (Stations UK)

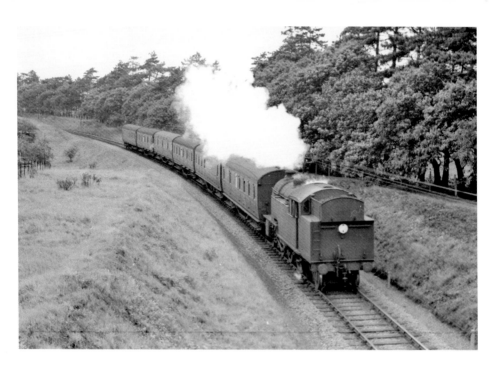

On 14 August 1957, this steam view shows a local passenger working consisting of six coaches, hauled by an unidentified Class L1 locomotive. This was seen near Derby Road station. (Brian Pask)

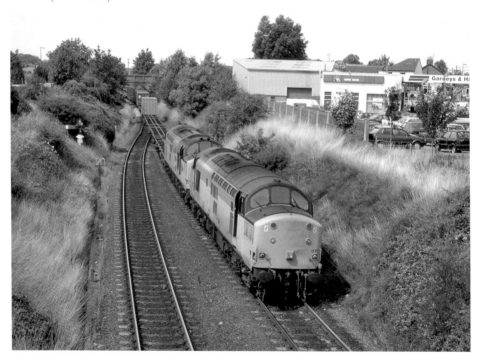

Some thirty-five years later, on 1 August 1992, a pair of Class 37s arrive at Derby Road station with the 05.04 Crewe to Felixstowe North service. (Ray Bishop)

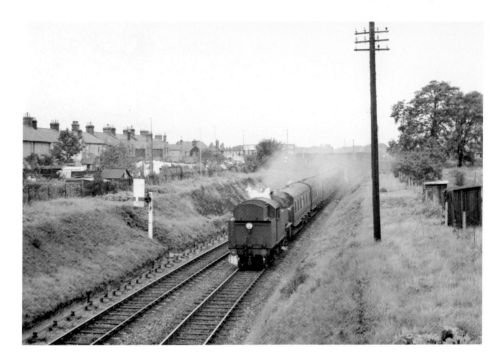

A Down direction Felixstowe branch working enters the loop at Derby Road with a steam-hauled passenger service. Motive power was again provided by a Class L1 tank locomotive. Note the short Up starting signal on the opposite bank, complete with sighting board. (Brian Pask)

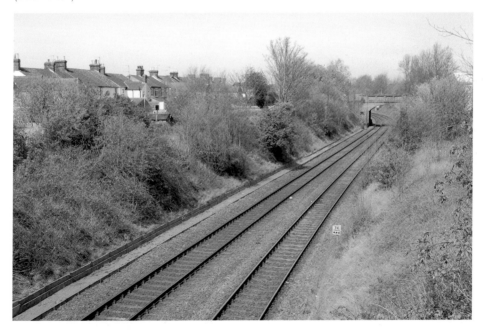

The same view today, looking back towards Westerfield, shows the houses on the left and considerable vegetation growth on the bank. The semaphore signal has gone, replaced with a colour light example near the next overbridge. (Ray Bishop)

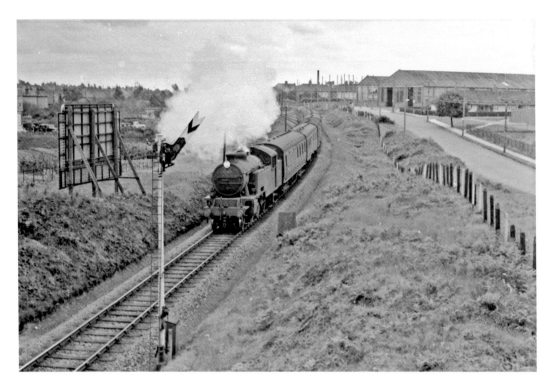

On 14 August 1957, an unidentified L1 tank engine passes Derby Road's Down distant signal, near to Ipswich trolleybus depot (now Ipswich Transport Museum). (Brian Pask)

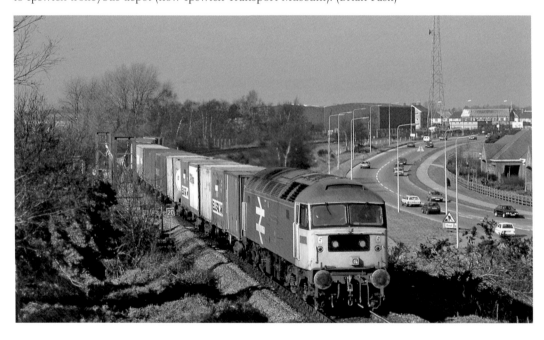

A Stratford to Felixstowe Freightliner service, hauled by 47007, is seen passing Nacton on 27 February 1988. This particular day featured sunshine and a blue sky – the photographer's ideal weather! (John Day)

Orwell

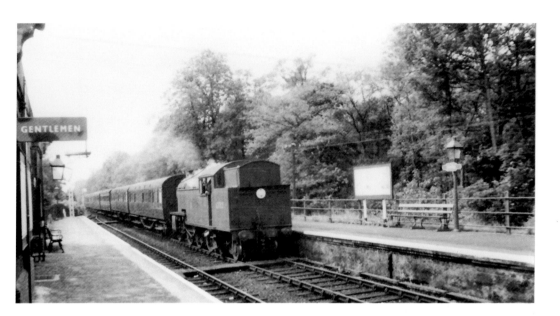

L1 tank engine No. 67717, running tender-first on a local Felixstowe passenger service, enters Orwell station in 1955. The track at this time was bullhead rail in chairs on wooden sleepers. (Stations UK)

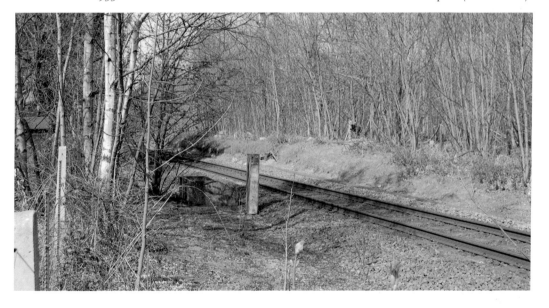

By standing on the remains of the Up platform, today's view shows only a mound of earth where the former Down platform was located. The single line now runs roughly down the centre of the formation. Today the track is continuous welded rail on concrete sleepers, able to handle the heaviest freight trains. (Ray Bishop)

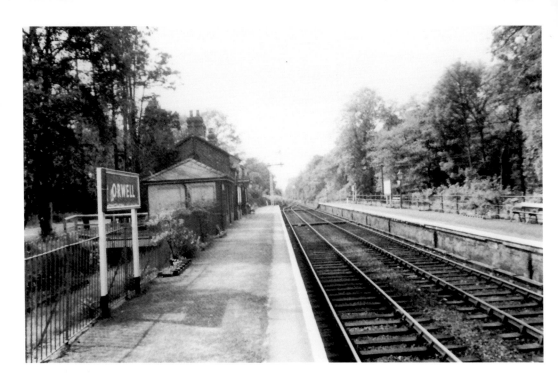

General view of Orwell station, showing the station buildings on the Up platform, the station name board, the Down platform, and the bracket signal protecting the single line towards Derby Road. This view was taken in 1955. (Stations UK)

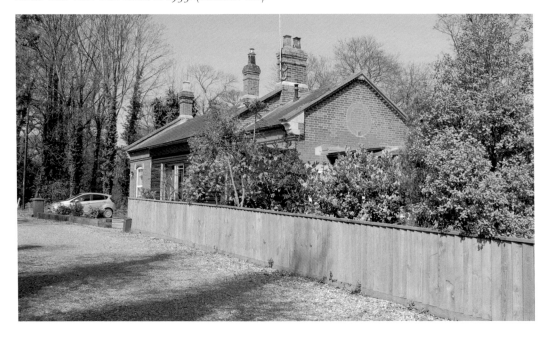

After the station closed completely on 15 June 1959, the station buildings were eventually sold off for conversion into a private house. The station buildings retain a lot of the original features. (Ray Bishop)

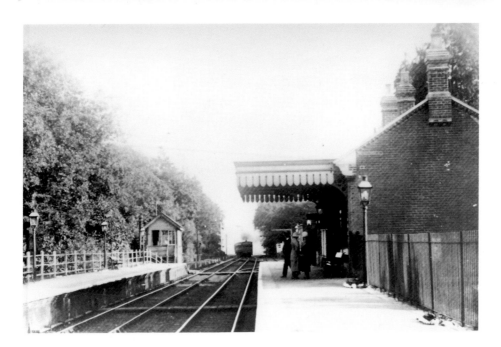

Orwell station opened when the line was constructed and was the principal crossing place on the branch for a number of years. In this view, we see a local passenger service arriving on the Up platform with a Felixstowe to Ipswich service in 1911. (HMRS ABB911)

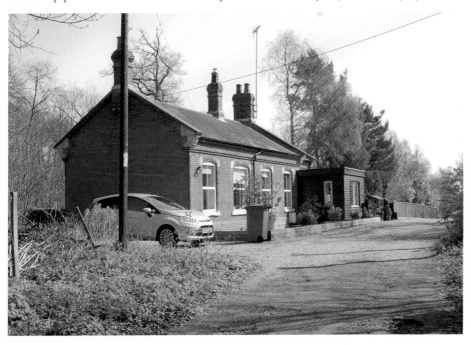

A slightly different view of Orwell Station, taken from the approach road during 2012, showing the original buildings complete with chimneys and decorative brickwork. A small extension has been added to the outside. The driveway used to lead to the former goods yard. (Ray Bishop)

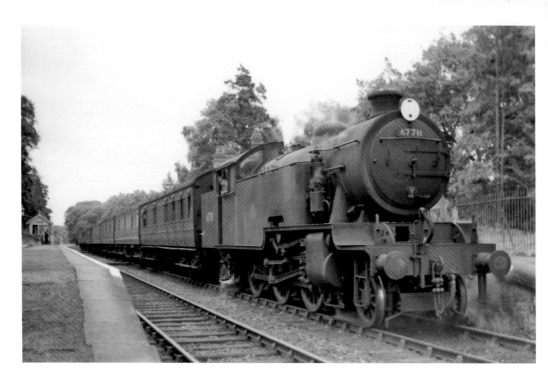

Locomotive Class L1 No. 67711, on an Up local passenger service, calls at Orwell during 1956. Loadings must have still been plentiful, as six passenger coaches were provided. (S. Summerson/Transport Treasury)

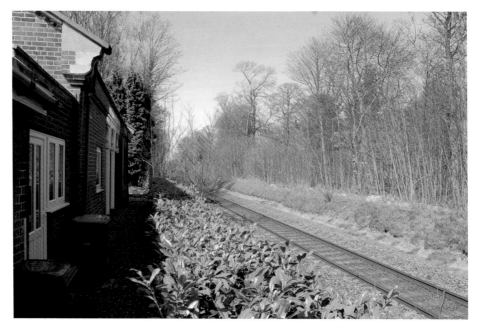

With permission of the owner, this view was taken from the platform side of the station buildings. A small portion of the platform has been retained. The laurel bushes hide the operational railway, a few feet away. (Ray Bishop)

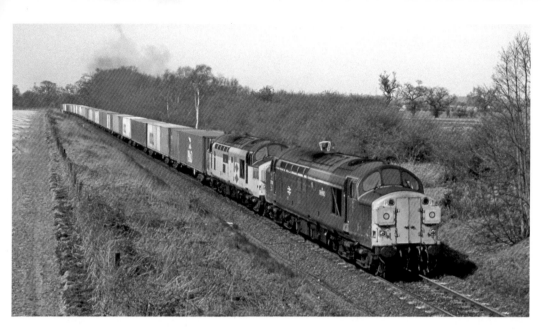

Between Orwell and Trimley, there is a level crossing at Levington. Originally a manned crossing with gates and protected by semaphore signals, it is now an automatic crossing and has always been a favoured spot for photographers. 37013 and 37015 are seen approaching the crossing on 29 March 1990, with a Felixstowe bound working. (John Day)

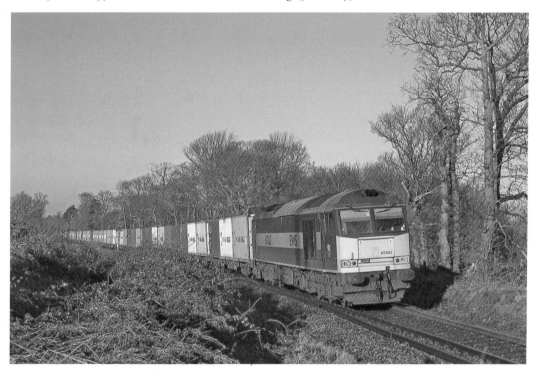

Moving forward just twenty-two years, we see Class 60062 hauling the 19.25 Scunthorpe to Felixstowe South Freightliner service, the date being 27 January 2007. (John Day)

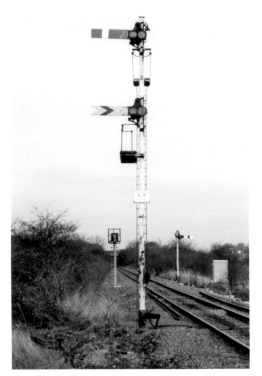

Signalling memories – the Up starter at Felixstowe Beach with the fixed distant below it. Note the board with the inscription 'Non Token Working Ahead'. The replacement colour light is seen in front of the signal, and the Down home signal for Felixstowe Beach is the signal on the right. (David Underwood)

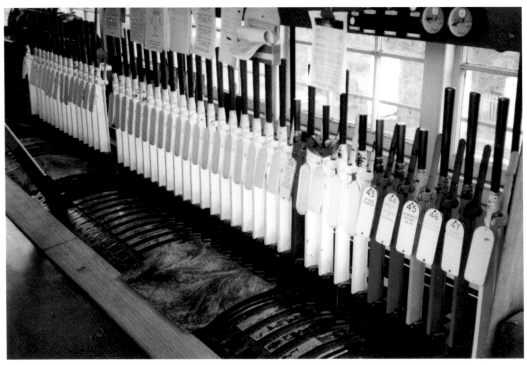

Inside view of Westerfield Junction signal box in its final form, showing many white spare levers. The lever frame was a McKenzie & Holland, of some forty-eight levers, originally installed in 1912. (David Underwood)

Trimley

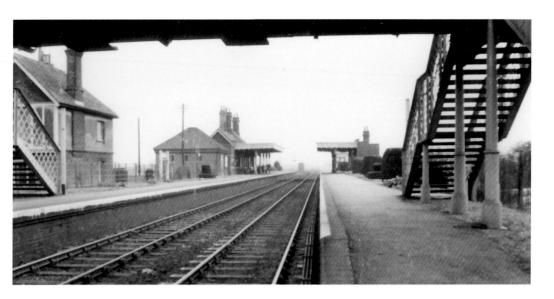

General view looking towards Felixstowe, taken from the Up platform in 1956. Note the clean and tidy appearance of the station. Solid brick buildings and canopies were provided on both platforms. (Stations UK)

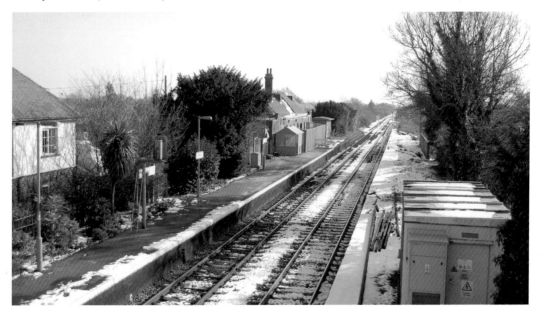

On a bright and cold morning this year, an elevated view of the station shows the changes over the last fifty-five years. Now only the far platform is in use for the passenger service – the former Up loop now forms the line to North Freightliner terminal at Felixstowe. (Ray Bishop)

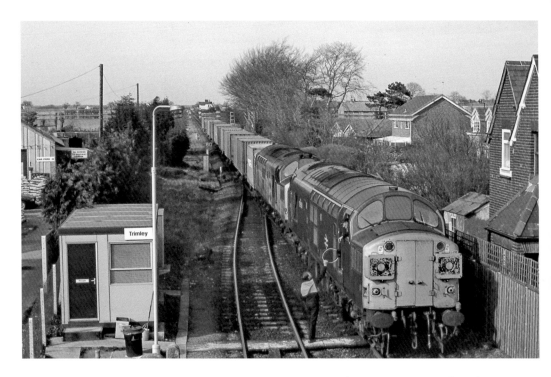

Diesel locomotives Nos 37009 and 37242 arrive at Trimley and surrender the token to the signalman. The train was 4Y70, the 10.09 Stratford to Felixstowe South Freightliner terminal, and this view was taken on 2 March 1990. (John Day)

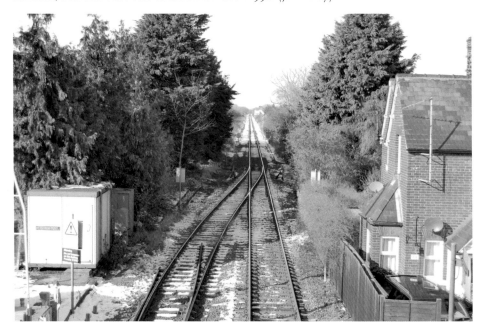

Moving on some twenty-two years, the trees have all grown up and the modern portacabin-type signal box has gone, replaced by the line-side signalling equipment building. The branch signalling and level crossing are now controlled from Colchester. (Ray Bishop)

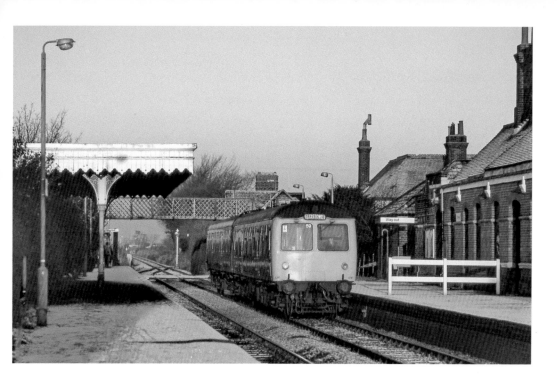

Cravens type DMU Nos 54416 and 53368 arrive on a local passenger working from Ipswich on 4 January 1986. Only the Ipswich end of the platform is now used. The canopy has been removed and the buildings are closed up. (John Day)

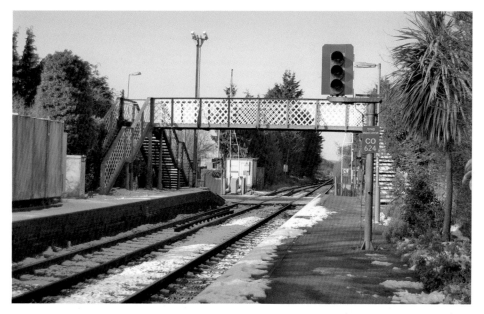

A view today from the passenger platform, looking at the level crossing – now controlled by CCTV from Colchester signalling centre. The signal in the foreground is a SPAD indicator; this only illuminates if the CO624 signal, located behind the photographer, is passed at Danger. (Ray Bishop)

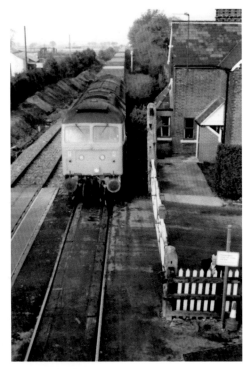

Class 47 enters the station on a Freightliner working to Felixstowe South. The level crossing at this time was manually operated by the signalman, who used to cycle down from the signal box, as by this time there were no other staff at the station. (Andy T. Wallis)

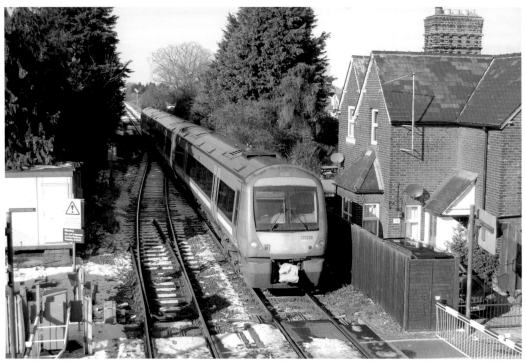

Today a Class 170 DMU, substituting for a failed Class 153, arrives at Trimley. The level crossing is now full barriers, controlled by CCTV. Trap points have been added to protect the single line towards Derby Road. (Ray Bishop)

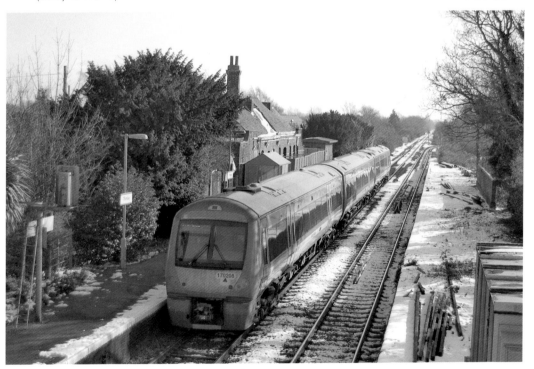

From February 1987, the former Up loop at Trimley closed and the line was designated an engineer's siding. While it was re-laid and connected to the new line that had been built from the North Freightliner depot, which opened in March 1987, the left-hand line was retained for passenger trains to Felixstowe and freight trains to the South Terminal. A Met/Camel DMU waits to proceed to Derby Road. (Andy T. Wallis)

Today the view sees a Class 170 DMU *en route* to Felixstowe. Note the station buildings are fenced off, pending an uncertain future; all the former buildings on the Up side have long gone. (Ray Bishop)

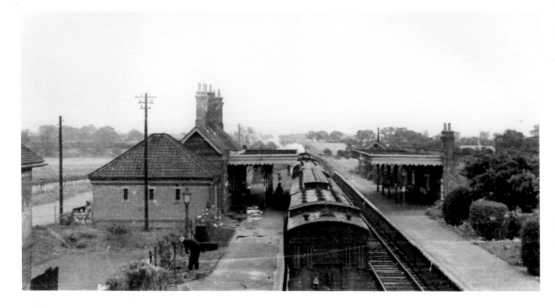

This view from the footbridge, looking towards Felixstowe, shows a steam passenger working in 1946. The station looks in splendid condition and fairly tidy following the ravages of the war years. (Stations UK)

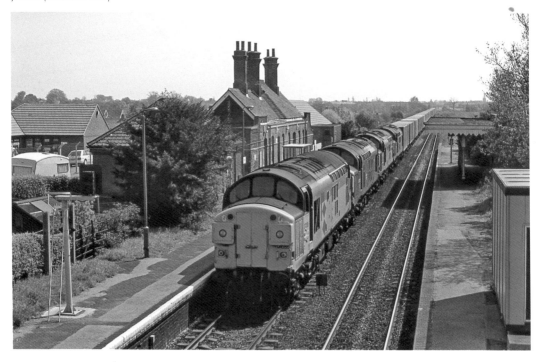

Superpower 1990s style! Normally a pair of Class 37s would handle the Freightliner trip workings to Ipswich yard, but due to limited paths over the single-line sections, the only way to get spare engines back to Ipswich was on the front of a booked working. The locomotives are 37055, 072, 059 and 077. The train is the 4Y81 Felixstowe South to Ipswich Yard service, and the date is 28 April 1990. (John Day)

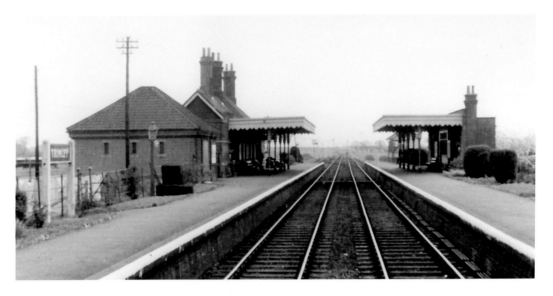

Trimley station viewed from the level crossing, as seen on 14 May 1956. The station is complete with its goods yard, buildings, and signal box. No doubt some passengers will appear when the next train is due. (H. C. Casserley)

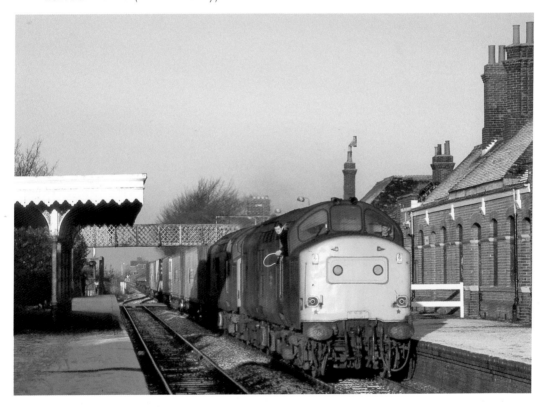

Rolling forward some thirty years sees a pair of Class 37s, Nos 168 and 148, arriving at the station on a Willesden to Felixstowe working. The second man is preparing to surrender the token for the single-line section from Derby Road. (John Day)

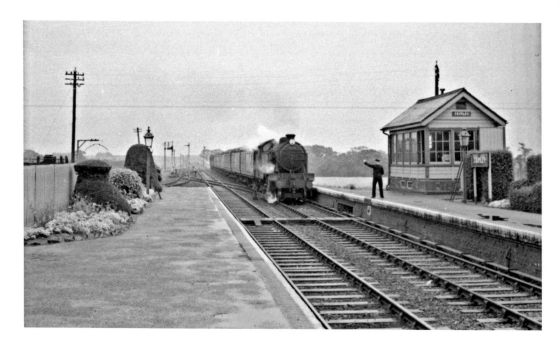

Locomotive Class L1 No. 67702 enters the station with an Up local service train to Ipswich on 12 August 1957. The signalman is waiting to receive the single-line token from Felixstowe Town to Trimley section. (Brian Pask)

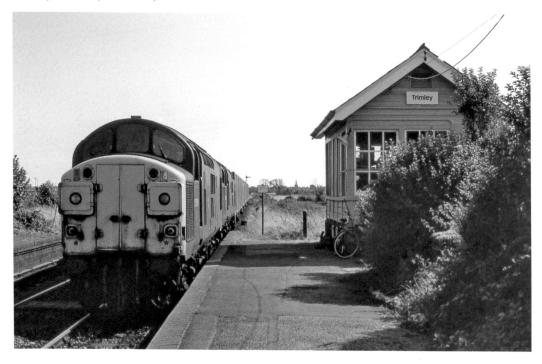

Moving on to 1985, 37089 arrives at Trimley Up loop, awaiting its path forward to Derby Road. The signalman's bike can be seen outside the front of the signal box, waiting for its next trip down to the level crossing gates. (John Day)

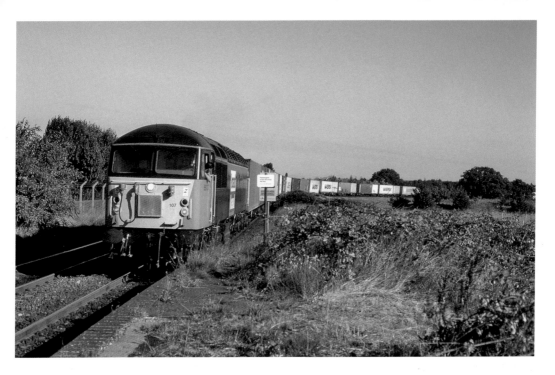

On a lovely August day, Class 56107 is seen entering Trimley station from Felixstowe North. The patch of ground in the foreground is where the old signal box once stood. (Ray Bishop)

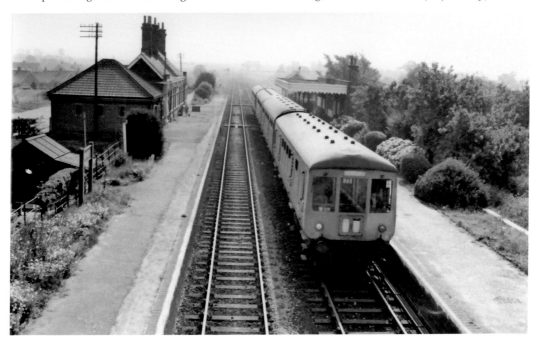

A four-car DMU arrives at Trimley, formed of Class 100 Gloucester units on the front set. The identity of the rear is not known. The date is between the mid-1960s and 1980, when these type of DMUs were withdrawn. (Dr I. C. Allen/Transport Treasury)

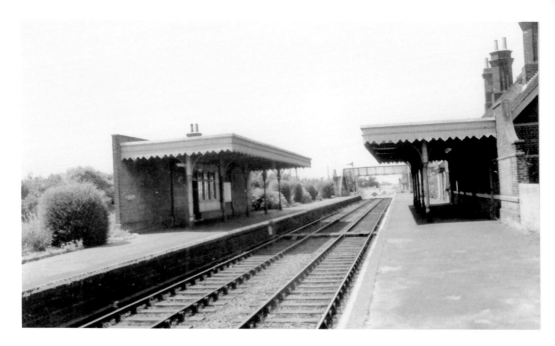

An unusual view of the station, looking back towards the level crossing in better times, with the station complete and looking cared for. This view was taken from the Felixstowe end of the Down platform. (Stations UK)

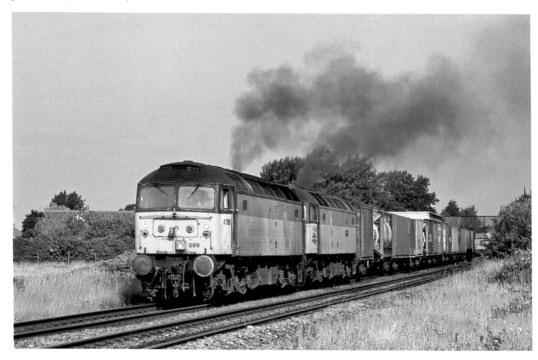

On 21 July 1995, locomotives 47399 and 47387 power away from Trimley with train 4L95, the 21.21 Coatbridge to Felixstowe North Freightliner service. The line in the foreground led to Felixstowe Town station and the south terminal. (John Day)

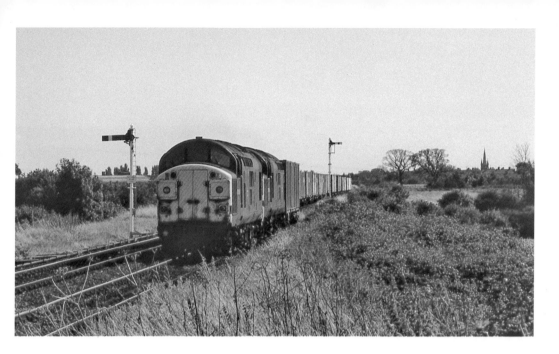

37089 leads another unidentified Class 37 into the loop at Trimley during 1985. Note the semaphore signals, which had a couple of more years' work before being replaced with colour light examples. (John Day)

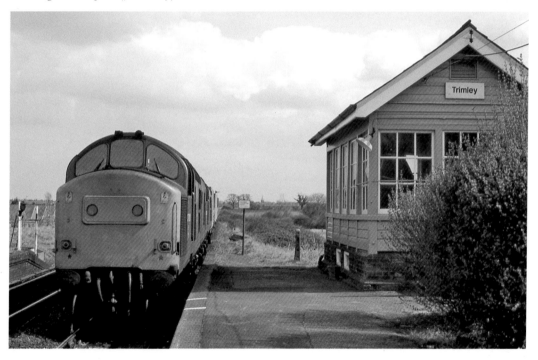

In the same year, another pair of Class 37s enter the loop at Trimley, past the signal box. The leading locomotive is 37091. These views were taken before work commenced on the new link to the North terminal. (John Day)

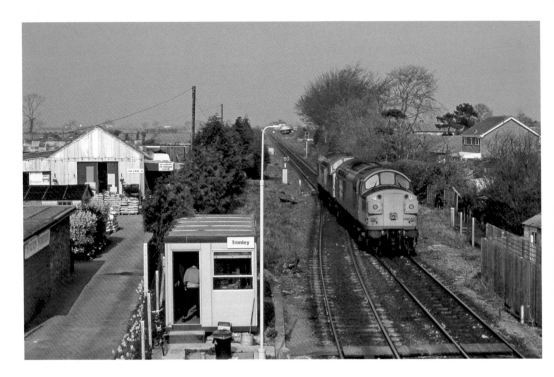

The original Trimley signal box was closed in 1987, when a new portacabin-type signal box was opened adjacent to the level crossing. Before this could happen, all the old semaphore signals had to be replaced with colour lights. A pair of Class 37s can be seen arriving at the station, having been signalled towards the South terminal. (John Day)

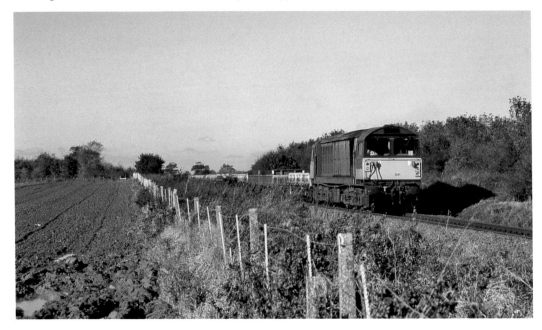

In preparation for the complete resignalling of the line in 1999, an engineer's train is seen on 1 November 1998 near Trimley, hauled by locomotive 58041. (John Day)

Felixstowe Town

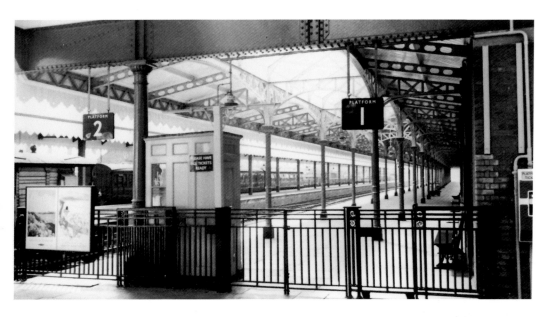

View taken from the station concourse, looking at the ticket barrier protecting platforms 1 and 2, taken in 1961. The station benefited from a wide concourse. The newer island platform can be seen in the background, with a set of coaches standing in platform 4 awaiting their next passenger turn. (Stations UK)

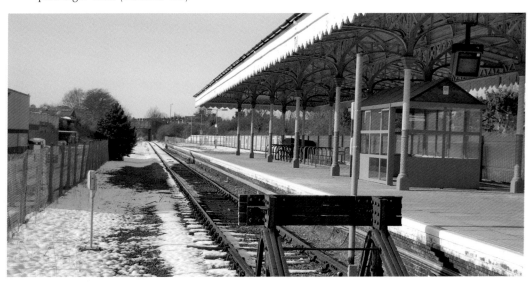

Some fifty plus years later, only a small portion of the original platform 2 is in use. The common feature of both photographs is the original canopy, still going strong in providing shelter from the elements. (Ray Bishop)

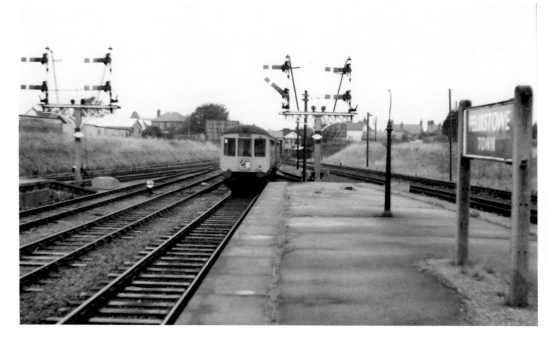

A Class 100 Gloucester type DMU departs from the Town station, signalled towards Ipswich in the late 1950s, before any rationalisation had affected to the layout at Felixstowe Town. (Dr I. C. Allen/Transport Treasury)

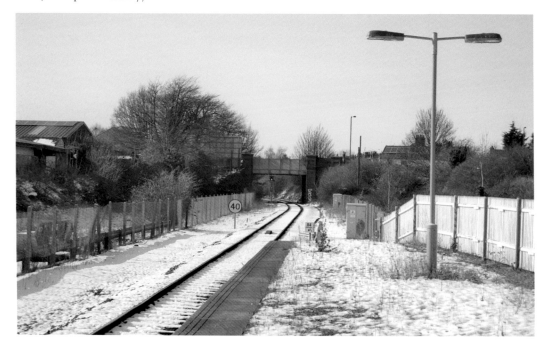

A wintry scene, looking off the end of the town platform towards Trimley and Ipswich. The former station signal box was located on the right, next to the road overbridge. The signal seen under the bridge is now controlled from Colchester Power signal box, as is the whole line. (Ray Bishop)

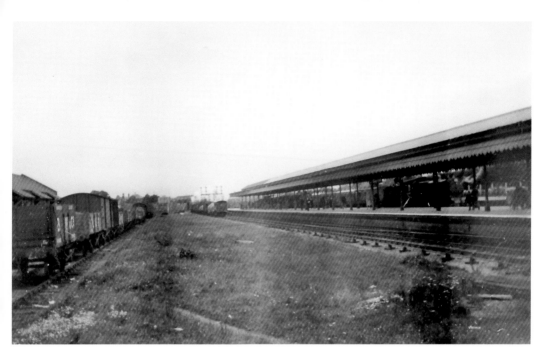

A 1928 LNER view, taken from the buffer stops end of the station, looking at the original island platform. The goods yard, with plenty of traffic, is on the left of the picture. The space in the middle is where the LNER built the new island platform – little did anybody know that it was only to last around thirty years, before the track was lifted. (Stations UK)

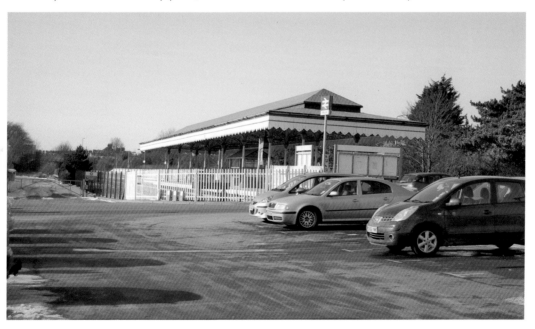

A small portion of the original island platform, with just one side in use, has been retained for the local train service. The remaining area has been given over to car parking and retail units. (Ray Bishop)

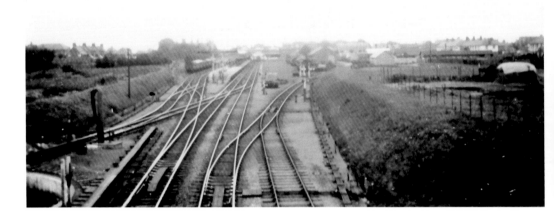

Early LNER view of the station, as seen from the road overbridge. At that time, platforms 3 and 4 did not exist. The loco depot is on the extreme left of the view, with the edge of the turntable just in view on the left. The carriage sidings were on the left in the far distance, and the goods yard is on the right of the picture. (Stations UK)

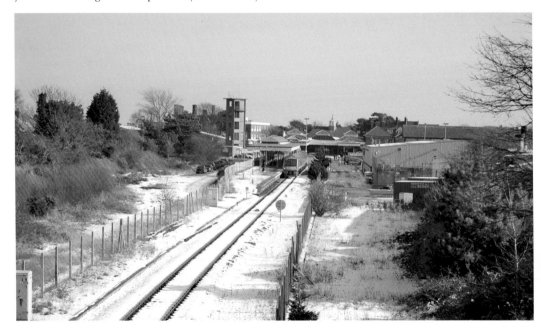

The same view today features just a short length of the original island platform in use. A fire station is built on the site of the carriage sidings, and a factory unit occupies part of the old goods yard. (Ray Bishop)

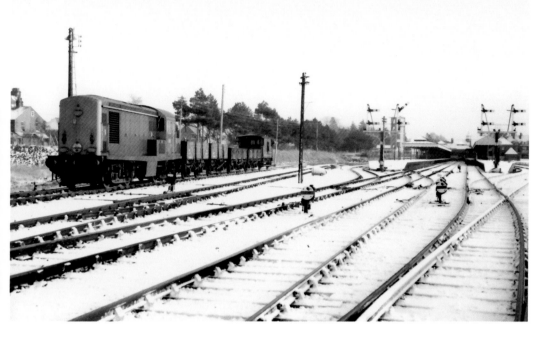

An early example of the British Railways modernisation plan saw 800 horsepower type 1 diesels, later classified as Class 15 shunting wagons, on a local goods working in the sidings at the town station. (Dr I. C. Allen/Transport Treasury)

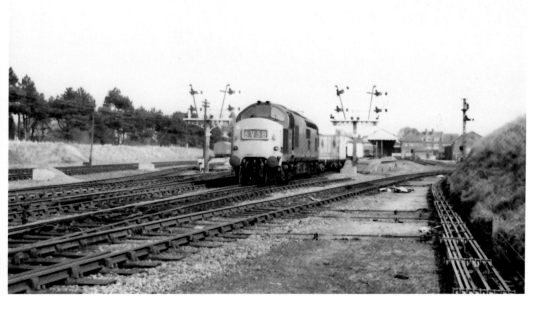

A few years later, a Class 37 works train 6V38 away from Felixstowe with a Freightliner working towards Felixstowe docks. By this time, the mid-1960s platform 4 and its run-round loop had already been taken out of use and the track lifted. (Dr I. C. Allen/Transport Treasury)

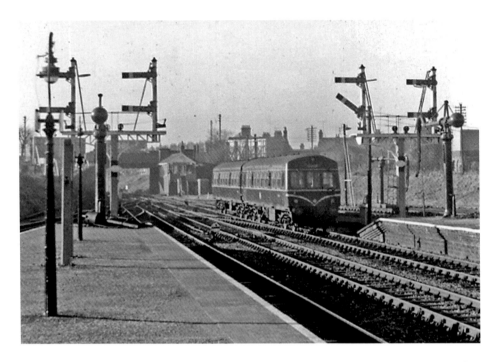

Early colour view of a Met/Camel DMU, departing with a train to Ipswich on 2 December 1961. Note the fine array of semaphore signals located on the platform end of the station. At this time, water cranes were provided on both platform ends for replenishing steam locomotives. (Brian Pask)

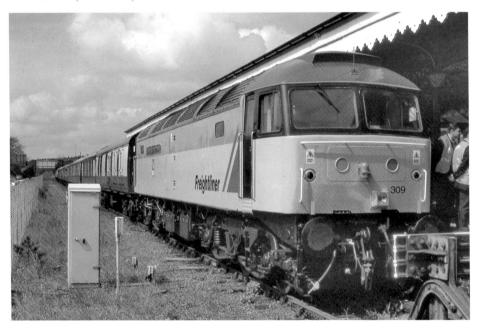

A special locomotive-hauled train, No. 47309, standing at the buffers at Felixstowe Town, having arrived from London. The train was run by Freightliner in connection with the naming of a locomotive. The train was topped and tailed with 47301 at the other end. (Ray Bishop)

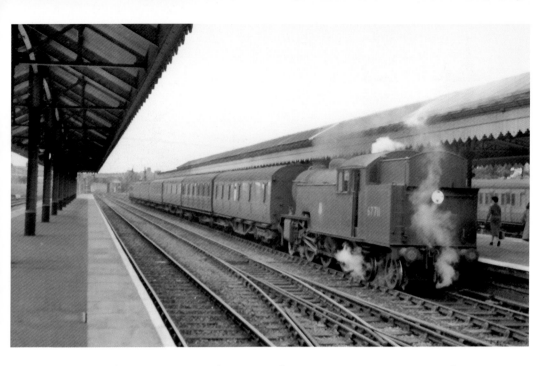

Tank engine Class L1 arrives at Felixstowe with a passenger train on 7 September 1956. Once uncoupled, the locomotive would draw forward and use the centre road to run round on. (A. Summersby/Transport Treasury)

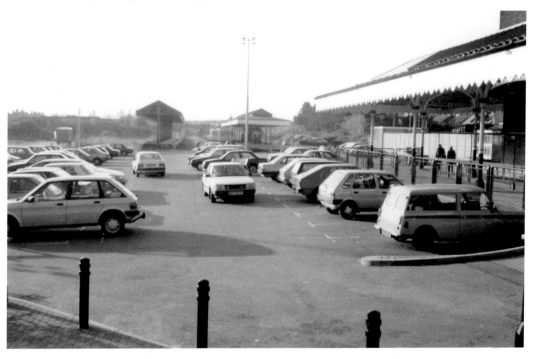

Some thirty years later the station had been reduced to a small piece of the island platform, seen in the distance, while the rest was given over to retail use and car parking. (Andy T. Wallis)

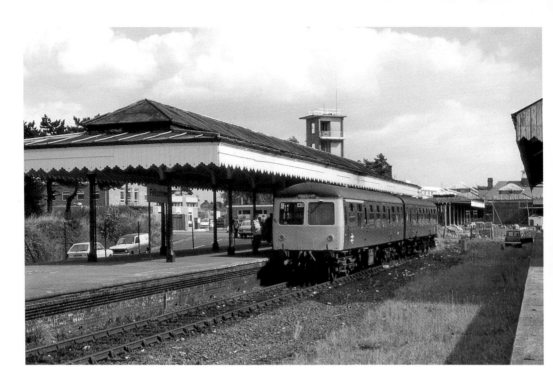

After the station became unstaffed, it was left to fall into disrepair until it was sold off for redevelopment. By 1984, work had commenced – a Cravens Class 105 DMU is seen standing at the recently truncated platform, while the area behind it is given over to the contractors. The main buildings are now known as Great Eastern Square. (John Day)

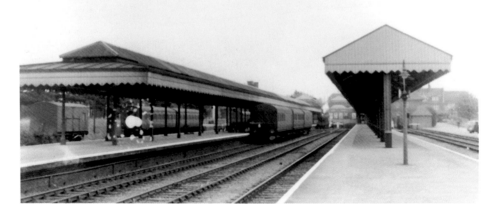

A similar view, taken from the other island platform on 14 May 1956. A train has arrived on platform two and the locomotive is preparing to run round its train. (H. C. Casserley)

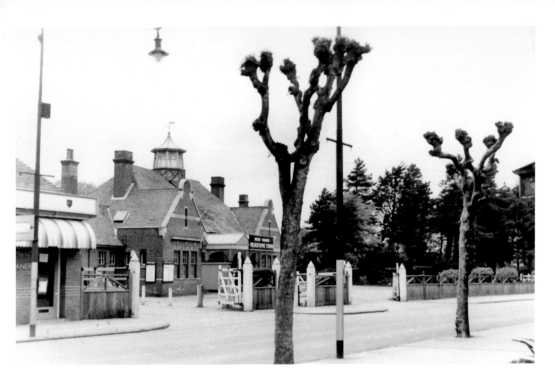

The town station seen from the road approach on 14 May 1965, with the dark blue 'British Railways Felixstowe Town' board on the front of the canopy. (H. C. Casserley)

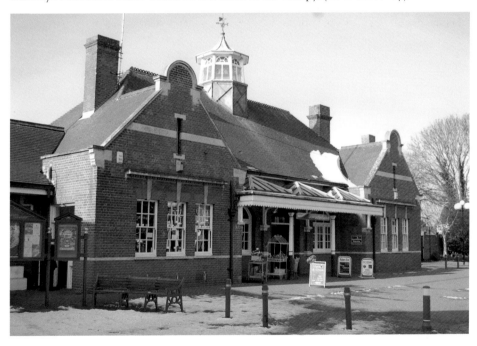

In February 2012, with the remains of earlier snowfall, the main buildings look in an excellent condition. The front canopy has been altered, but everything else remains the same – except it's not a station any more! (Ray Bishop)

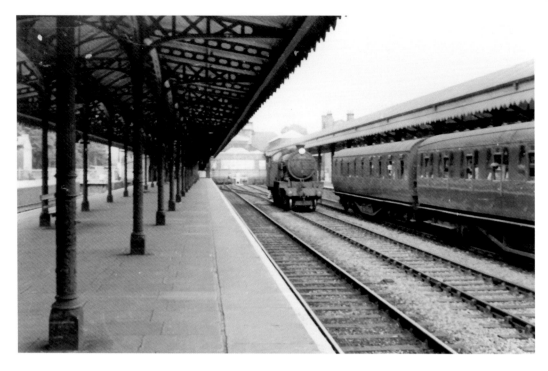

A unidentified tank engine runs round its coaches in platform 3 at the town station in 1959. Not long after this view was taken, DMUs took over the local passenger workings. (Stations UK)

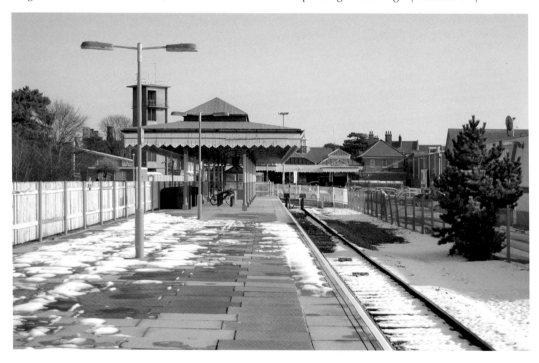

The view along the remaining part of the platform, looking towards the main buildings and Great Eastern Square. New fencing and platform lighting had also been provided. (Ray Bishop)

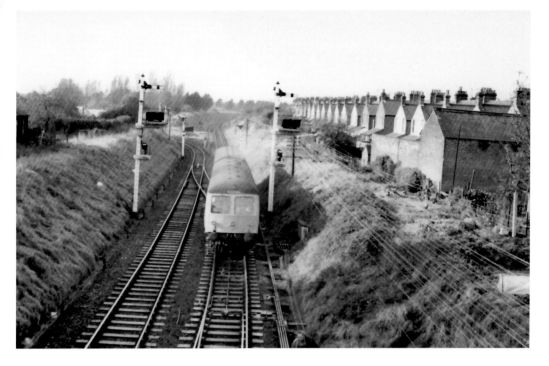

A Cravens Class 105 DMU departs towards Ipswich in this pre-1970 view from the road overbridge. In March 1970, all the semaphore signals were swept away when the signal box closed. (Dr I. C. Allen/Transport Treasury)

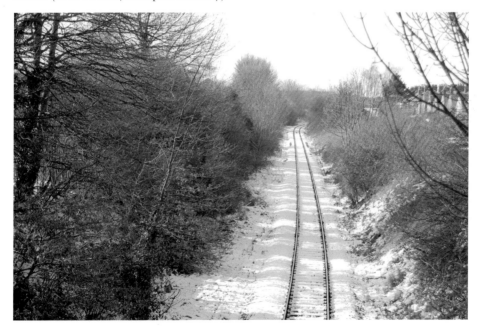

This year, all that remains is a single line going towards Trimley. All the signalling was taken out of use in 1970. Common to both views are the houses on the left. Vegetation clearance by Network Rail is obviously not a priority! (Ray Bishop)

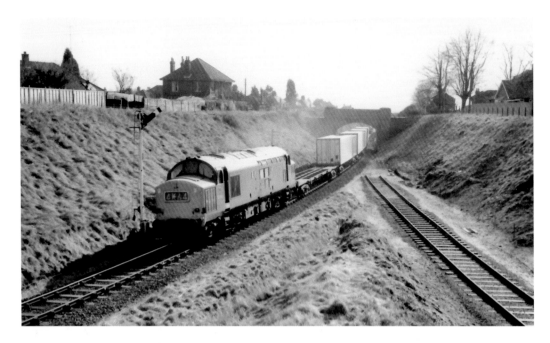

Prior to 1970, all traffic from the docks had to reverse at the town station before continuing its journey. A Class 37 is seen approaching the town station. The track on the right is the reinstated direct line, missing out the town station, closed since 1898. (Dr I. C. Allen/Transport Treasury)

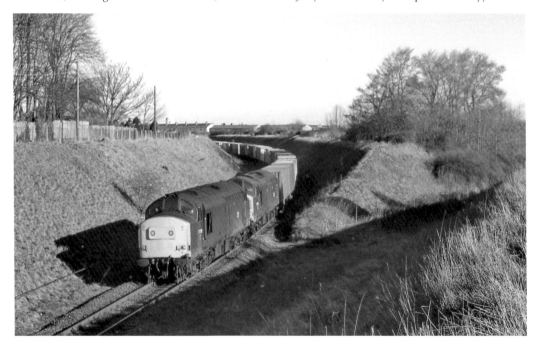

Taken from the bridge seen in the top view, we see 37091 and 37016 with a Felixstowe docks train, travelling over the west/south curve once more on 2 April 1985. The original line round to the town station can be seen on the right. Today the majority of the land in the former triangle, including the redundant formation to the town station, has been built on. (John Day)

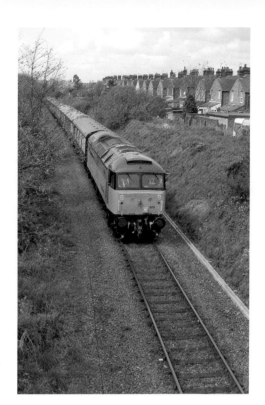

The special Freightliner train is seen arriving at Felixstowe Town, with 47309 leading and 47301 on the other end as there were no run-round facilities at the town station. (Ray Bishop)

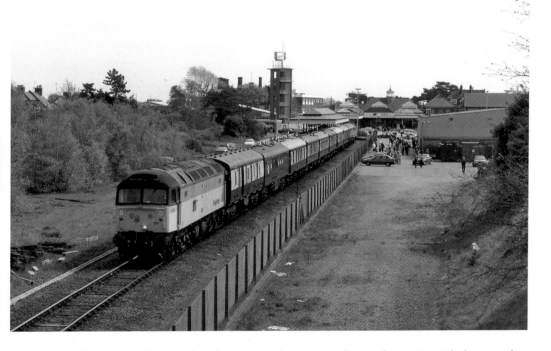

Viewed from the road overbridge, the train can be seen standing at the station with three coaches off the platform. This train was run by Freightliner in connection with a naming ceremony. The date was 22 April 1998. (Ray Bishop)

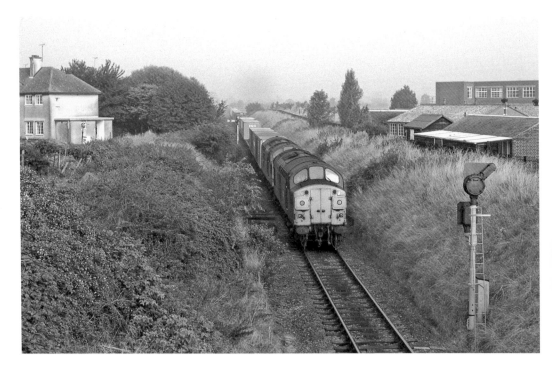

37089 and 37001 arriving at Felixstowe Beach Junction with a train for the south Terminal. The signal in the foreground routes to the former Beach station, or turns left for the Town station. (John Day)

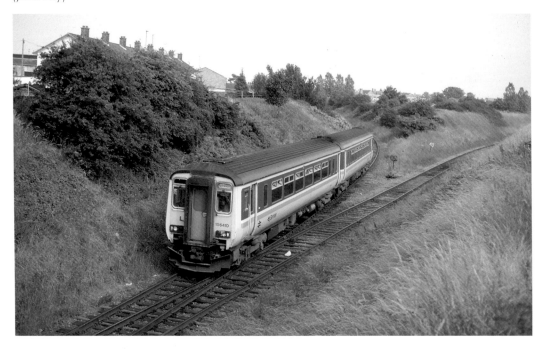

On 2 July 1993, unit 156410 negotiates Beach Junction on a return working back towards Ipswich. The line to the right is the reinstated direct link to the docks. (Ray Bishop)

Felixstowe Beach

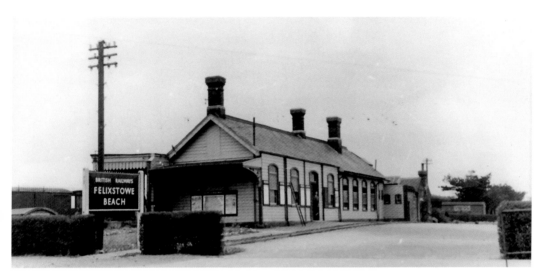

A nice, tidy and clear view of the exterior of the station buildings, taken on the 14 May 1956. Note the large enamelled 'British Railways Felixstowe Beach' sign, and also the lack of motor vehicles. (H. C. Casserley)

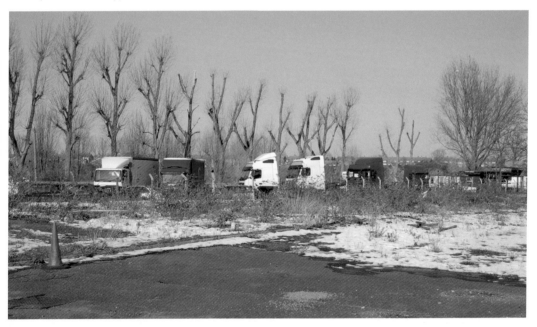

Today only the tarmac remains. The line of stunted trees and parked lorries is on the other side of the single-track railway. The buildings were demolished after they had been vacated, having been sublet to businesses for a number of years. (Ray Bishop)

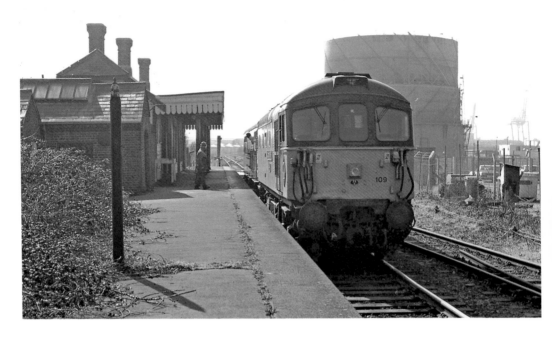

33109, propelling coach 975025, stands at the former Beach station with a special working – the 10.18 from Liverpool Street to Felixstowe Creek sidings – on 12 March 1996. (John Day)

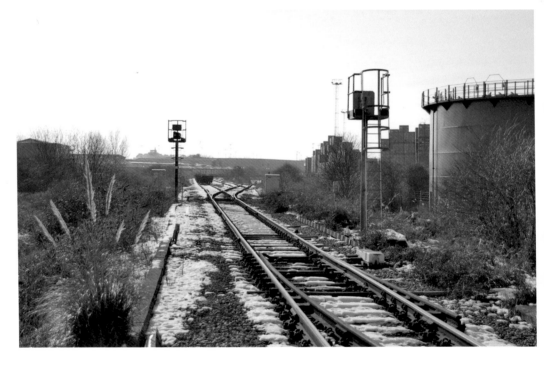

On the other side of the level crossing can be seen the line leading to the south terminal, and on the right that to Creek Sidings. The new colour light signals can be seen. The common feature in both photographs is the gas holder. (Ray Bishop)

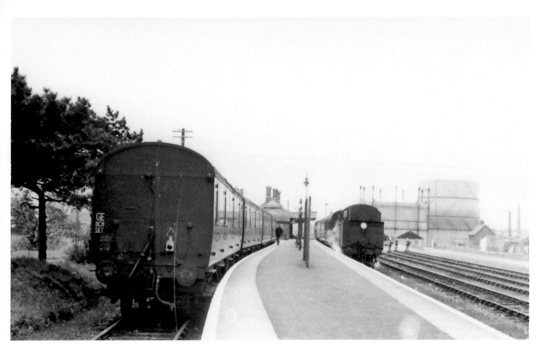

Locomotive Class L1 No. 67739 waits at the main platform for departure time. At this time the train would travel to Felixstowe Town, and the locomotive would run round the coaches for the journey to continue to Ipswich. A spare set of coaches occupies the bay platform, named GE branch set. (H. C. Casserley)

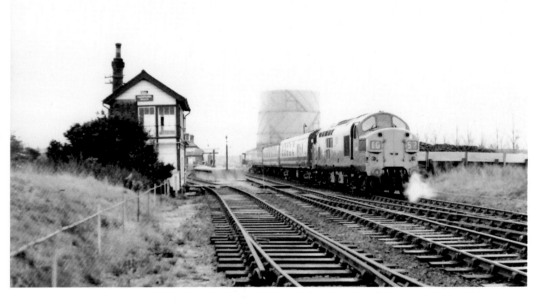

After 1967, the summer-only passenger service to the Beach station was withdrawn. An excursion set of coaches, plus locomotive D6733, stands in the siding. The signal box on the right had by this time closed, and the remaining points had been converted to hand operation. (Dr I. C. Allen/ Transport Treasury)

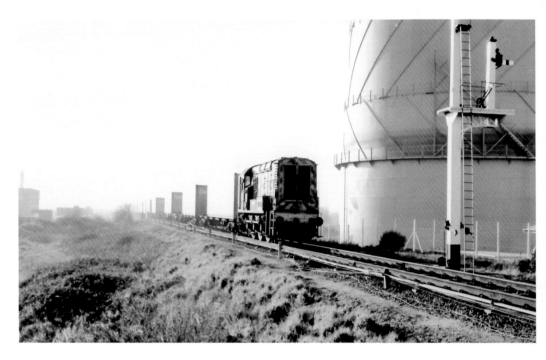

A Class 08 shunter is seen shunting a Freightliner set, as viewed from the level crossing at the Beach station. The wooden semaphore signal, seen on the edge of the picture, survived for a number of years before being replaced with a tubular steel signal and an elevated mechanical shunting signal, 'Dodd'. (Dr I. C. Allen/Transport Treasury)

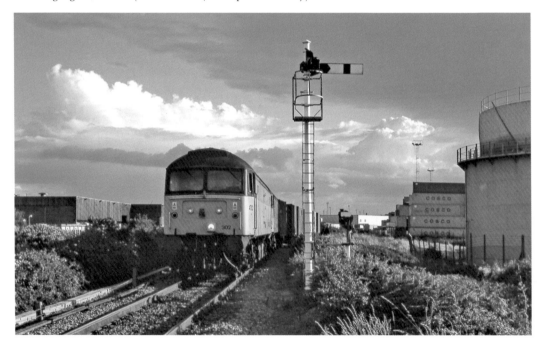

47302 and 47150 wait for the signal to precede with train 4E60, the 19.15 Felixstowe South to Wilton working, on 13 July 1998. (John Day)

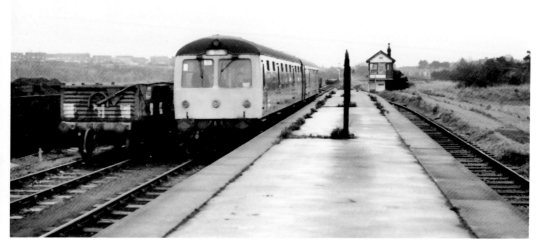

A two-car Cravens DMU stands at the Beach station with a pre-1967 working. Signs of neglect are already showing along the platform edge; the lampposts had already lost their lights. (Dr I. C. Allen/Transport Treasury)

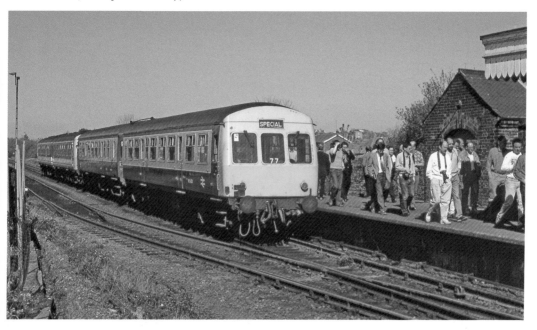

Many years later, on 15 April 1989, a double Met/Camel DMU visits the Beach station with the Branch Line Society's Rail tour, named the 'Orwell Docker'. Your author had the pleasure of travelling on this train. (John Day)

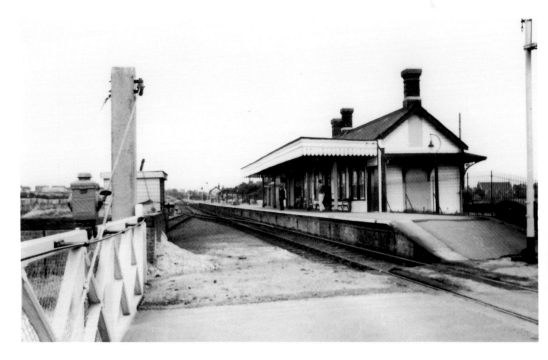

A view taken in 1961, looking from the gated level crossing, shows the station to be neat and tidy, complete with sidings and signal box. (Stations UK)

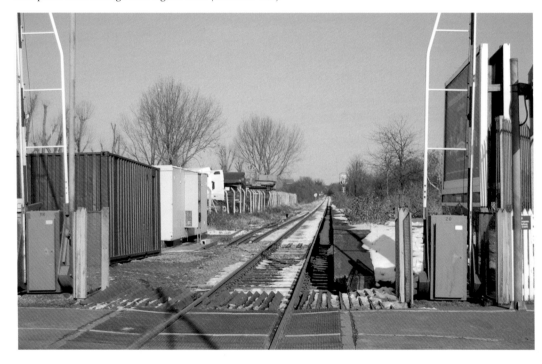

Some fifty-one years later all has changed, with the station buildings demolished and sidings lifted, with just the single line leading down to the Port of Felixstowe. The level crossing is now full barriers, controlled with the aid of CCTV from Colchester signalling centre. (Ray Bishop)

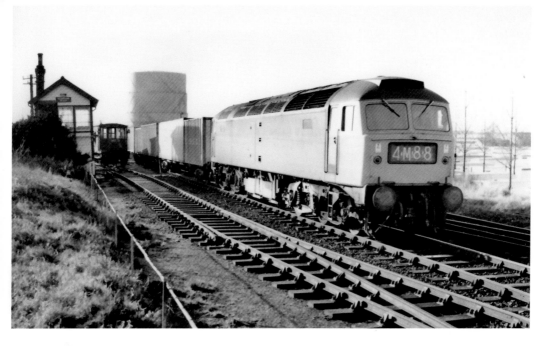

Class 47 departs with 4M88 Freightliner service from Felixstowe Docks, date unknown. The old signal box had by this time closed. (Dr I. C. Allen/Transport Treasury)

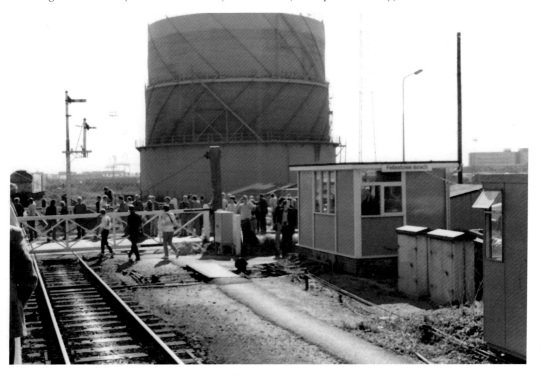

View from the platform after the Branch Line Societies special had arrived. The replacement signal box, a covered ground frame, is seen on the right. (Andy T. Wallis)

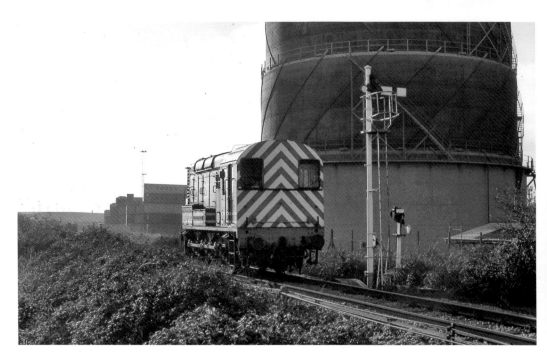

Former BR Class 10 shunter No. D3489, named after 'Colonel Tomline', the Felixstowe line's early benefactor, stands at the terminal side of Felixstowe Beach level crossing at the signal, waiting for its next shunting move. (Ray Bishop)

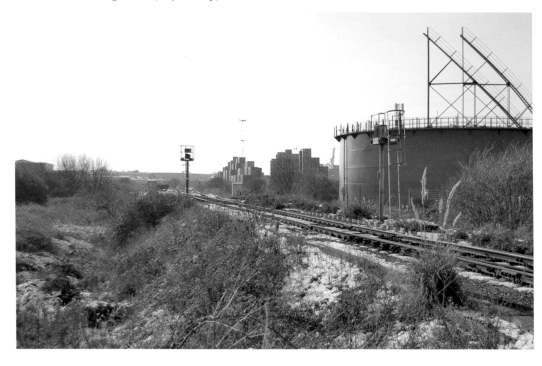

Today the same view shows a modern signal and a much-depleted gas holder. In the background can be seen stacked containers at the south terminal. (Ray Bishop)

Felixstowe Pier

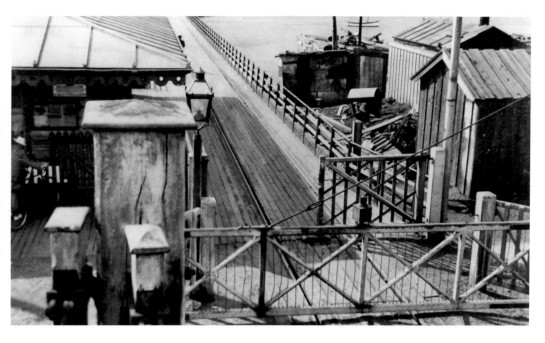

The original pier, seen from an elevated position in 1911. At this time the railway tracks continued beyond the station to the pier end. (HMRS ABB620)

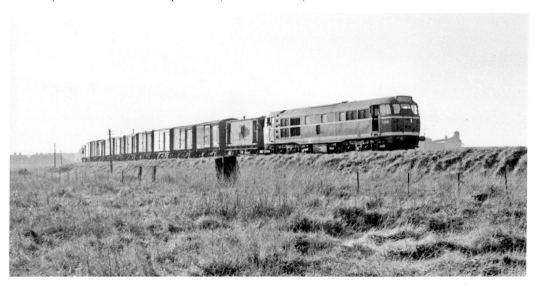

On 2 December 1961, an unidentified Class 31 diesel hauls a train of box vans, seen here between the Pier and Beach stations. Note the train has brake vans on both ends, ready for the run-round at the Town station. (Brian Pask)

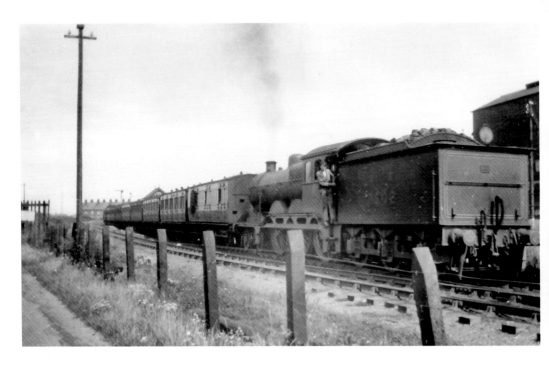

Locomotive B12 No. 8502 waits to depart from the Pier station with a passenger working. This view is dated *c.* 1928. (Stations UK)

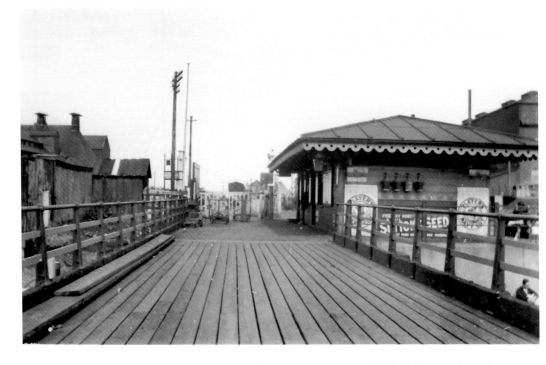

A view, also *c.* 1928, from the pier, looking back at the Pier station. The building on the right is the same as the 1911 view on page 83, but the railway tracks no longer continue along the actual pier. (Stations UK)

Felixstowe Docks
and Container Port

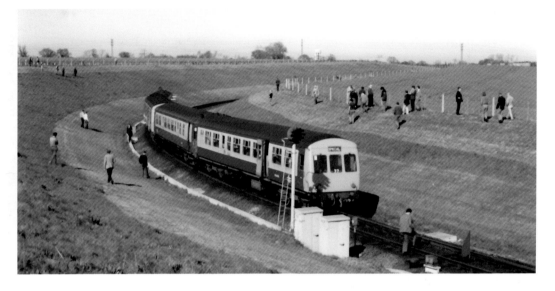

A Branch Line Society special DMU train visits the new north terminal at Felixstowe. The DMU was allowed to proceed as far as the edge of the complex, then the passengers were allowed to disembark to take the photographs. This view was taken on 15 April 1989. (Andy T. Wallis)

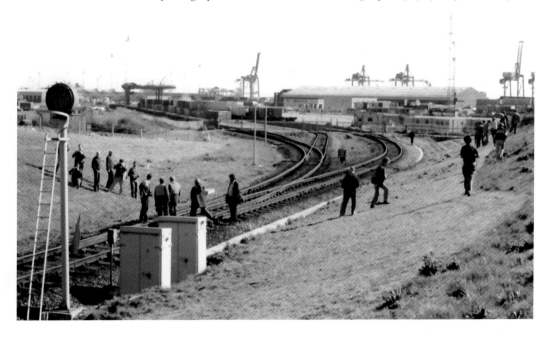

Another view, taken on the same day looking at the terminal, which had only been open for two years. (Andy T. Wallis)

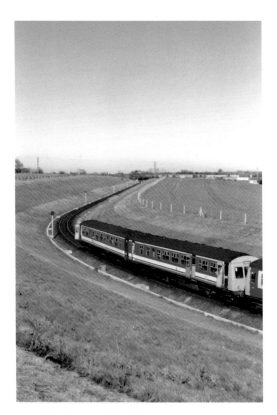

Some more views of the special, featuring the rear unit of the Met/Camel pair. The weather was bright but cold. The line beyond the unit leads back to Trimley. (Andy T. Wallis)

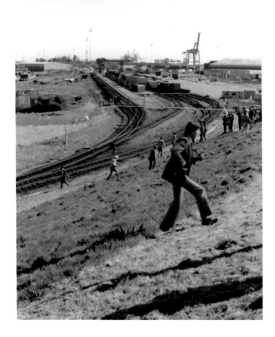

The passengers from the special were allowed to disembark to take photographs from the line-side before the DMU departed back towards Ipswich. (Andy T. Wallis)

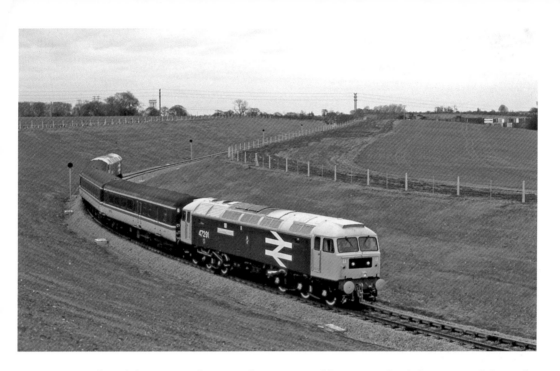

Opening day of the new north terminal saw a special locomotive-hauled train travel down the new line. The train was hauled by 47291 and was named at the opening ceremony. The date was 2 March 1987. (John Day)

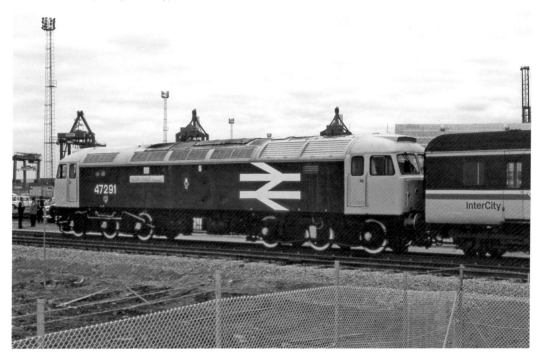

Close-up view of the locomotive to be named, 47291. It had obviously been given a good clean-up prior to the ceremony. (John Day)

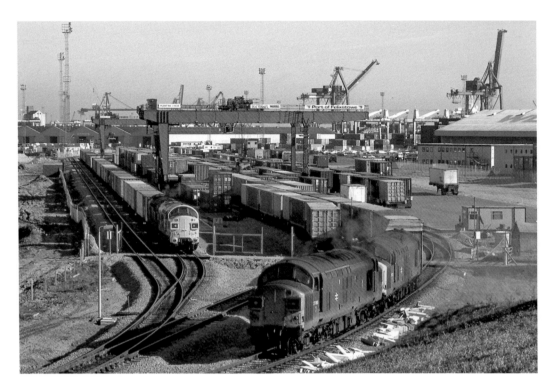

Just a couple of months later the depot was a hive of activity, with 37060 and 37221 waiting to depart with train 4L50, the 18.00 Felixstowe North to Leeds service train. Also in the view are 37116 and 37052. (John Day)

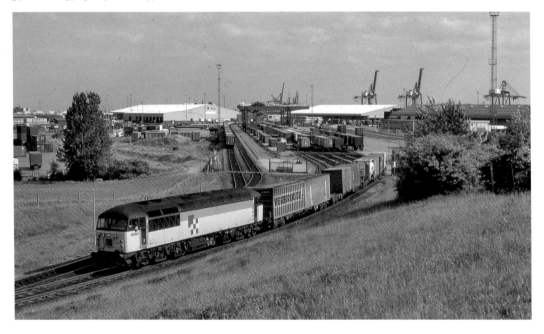

On 12 June 1996, the Class 37s had gone and motive power was a single Class 56. Here we see 56065 departing from the north terminal. (Ray Bishop)

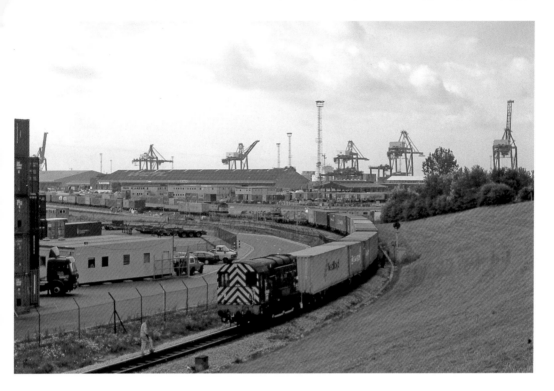

On 23 July 1998, the terminal pilot shunter moves container flat wagons to make up another working. The locomotive is 08642. Since the early views were taken, a new road behind the shunter has been built. (John Day)

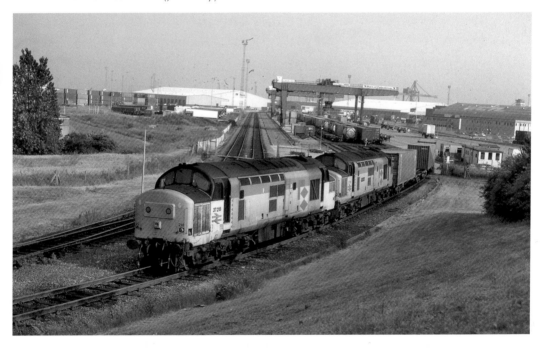

Five years previously, 37218 and 37261 shunt a train within the depot on 2 July 1993. (Ray Bishop)

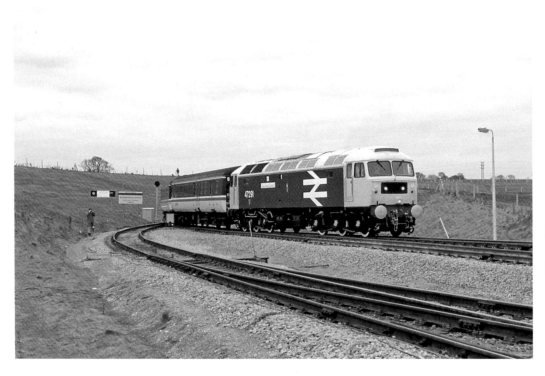

Another pair of views of the opening day special train which was to be named, first seen arriving with 47291 at the terminal, and later that day with 47585 leading proceedings back towards Trimley, with the engine now duly named, on 2 March 1987. (John Day)

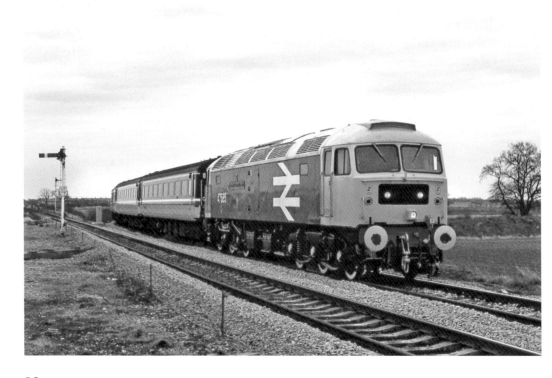

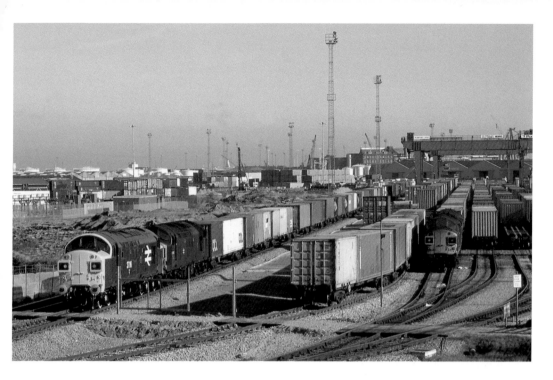

On 7 May 1987, 37116 and 37052 prepare to depart with another fully loaded working. (John Day)

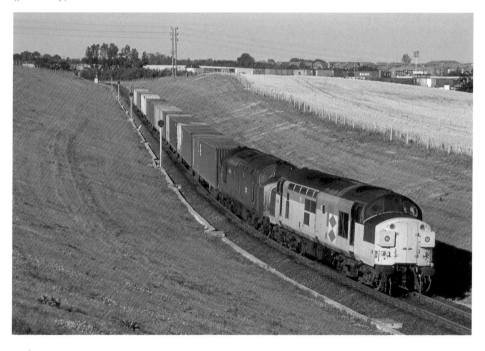

A pair of Class 37s arrive at the terminal with a short train of containers. 37063 is the leading locomotive, and Network Rail could learn a lot from terminal operators in line-side vegetation management! (John Day)

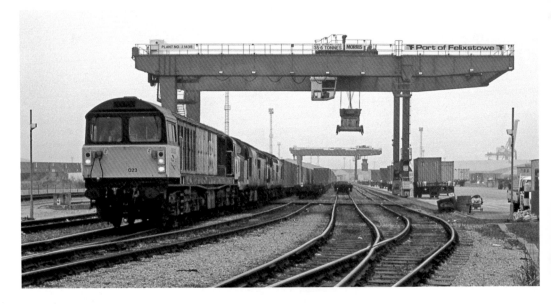

Class 58s saw some work on the branch in the 1990s. Here, 58023 prepares to depart with 4M47, the 11.20 Felixstowe North to Crewe working. A spare pair of 37s are tucked in behind the train engine getting a lift back to Ipswich yard. The date was 2 November 1993. (John Day)

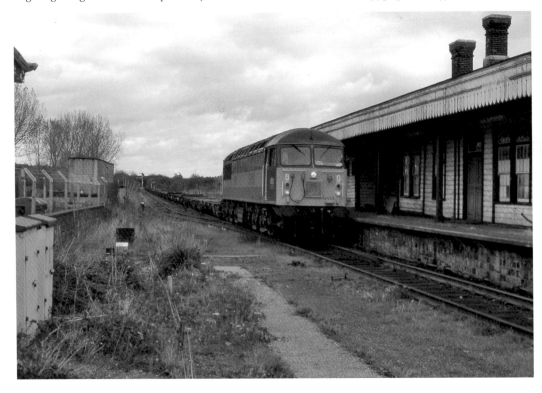

During the early 1990s, traffic to the south terminal dwindled to just two booked trains a day, plus light engine movements. In November 1997, a rake of empty Freightliner flats arrives at Felixstowe Beach, hauled by 56068. (Ray Bishop)

Branch Line Memories

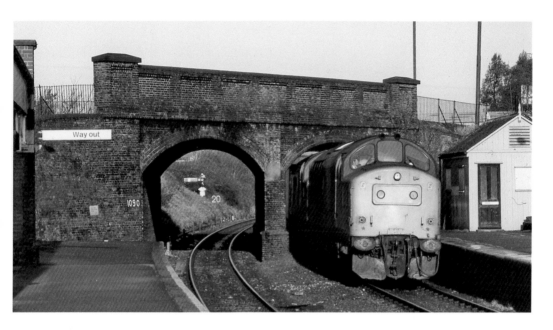

The old brick overbridge at Derby Road survived for more than 100 years before it had to be substantially rebuilt to take wider container traffic on the branch. 37178 leading 37100 into Derby Road station clearly shows the limited clearance there was. (John Day)

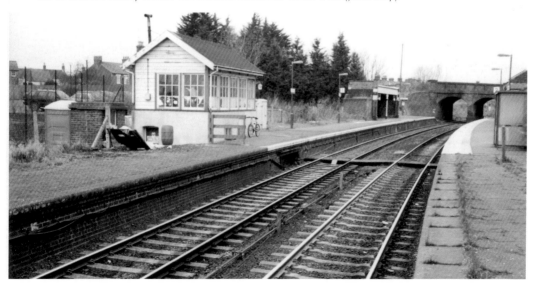

Derby Road signal box, seen in January 1999, shortly before it was closed and demolished. The box opened c. 1891 and was equipped with a McKenzie & Holland twenty-three-lever, five-inch centre frame. (David Underwood)

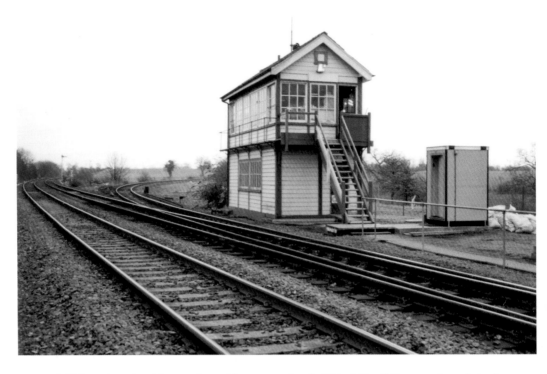

Westerfield Junction signal box and outside 1990s toilet facilities! The Felixstowe branch is the line curving away to the right. This view was taken in January 1999, shortly before the signal box was closed and demolished. (David Underwood)

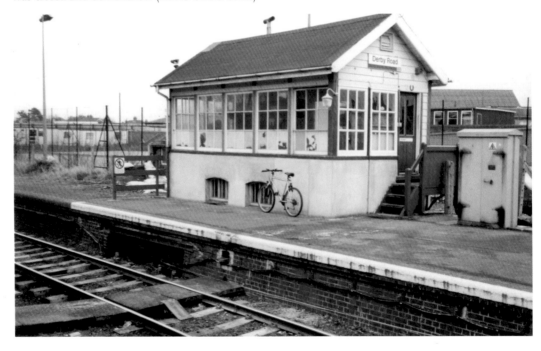

Another view of Derby Road signal box, with the signalman's bike parked outside. View taken in January 1999. (David Underwood)

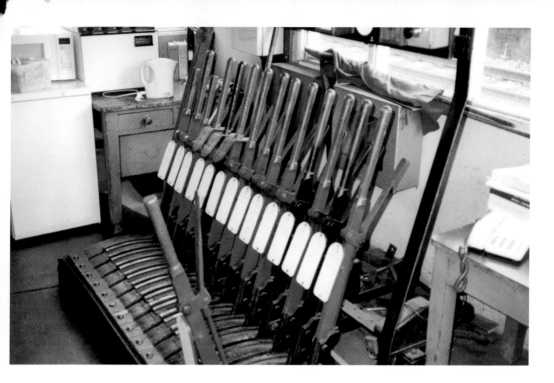

Inside view of the frame in Felixstowe Beach signal box, taken in January 1999 shortly before closure. The signal protecting the level crossing had already been replaced with a colour light, as had the gates with barriers. The siding opposite the platform had already been taken out of use. (David Underwood)

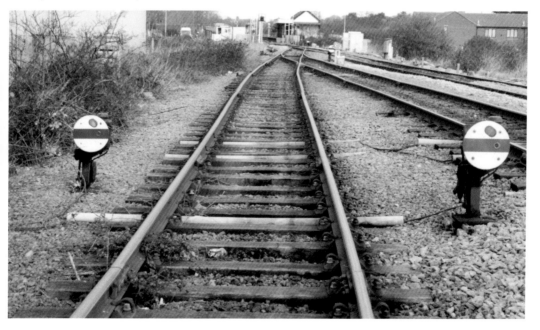

The mechanical Dodd's, protecting the exit from the Creek sidings, seen in January 1999. These fine signals would soon be replaced with modern equivalents. (David Underwood)

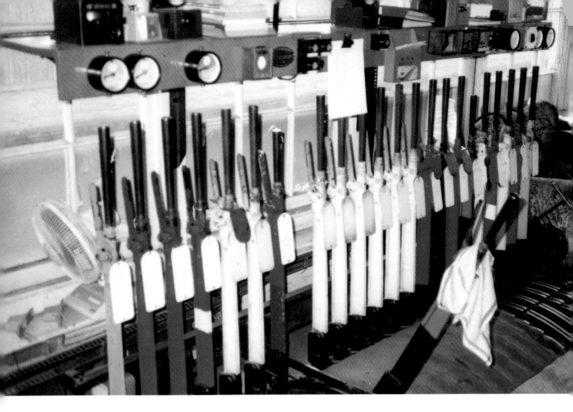

Interior of Derby Road Signal box, showing the twenty-three-lever McKenzie & Holland lever frame towards the end of its working life; the frame dated from 1891. Investment in new signalling by Railtrack in the late 1990s led to the closure of all the remaining signal boxes on the branch, with control then being from a new panel in Colchester Power Box. (David Underwood)

Acknowledgements

Special thanks to Ray Bishop and John Day for the provision of the modern images and for some of the earlier archive views. Once again, many thanks to Richard Casserley for allowing access to his photographic collection and to Brian Pask, Paul Lemon, David Underwood, and Dickie Pearce for help with the archive photographs. Thanks also to all the other photographers and organisations that have provided views from their collections. Finally, special thanks to the owner of Orwell station for allowing photographs to be taken on their property.